Teaching ESL/EFL
Listening and Speaking

Using a framework based on principles of teaching and learning, this guide for teachers and teacher trainees provides a wealth of suggestions for helping learners at all levels of proficiency develop their listening and speaking skills and fluency. By following these suggestions, which are organized around four strands—meaning-focused input, meaning-focused output, language-focused learning, and fluency development—teachers will be able to design and present a balanced programme for their students.

Teaching ESL/EFL Listening and Speaking, and its companion text, *Teaching ESL/EFL Reading and Writing*, are similar in format and the kinds of topics covered, but do not need to be used together. Drawing on research and theory in applied linguistics, their focus is strongly hands-on, featuring

- easily applied principles,
- a large number of useful teaching techniques, and
- guidelines for testing and monitoring.

All Certificate, Diploma, Masters and Doctoral courses for teachers of English as a second or foreign language include a teaching methods component. The texts are designed for and have been field tested in such programs.

I. S. P. Nation is Professor of Applied Linguistics in the School of Linguistics and Applied Language Studies at Victoria University in Wellington, New Zealand.

Jonathan Newton is a senior lecturer in the School of Linguistics and Applied Language Studies, Victoria University in Wellington, New Zealand.

ESL & Applied Linguistics Professional Series
Eli Hinkel, Series Editor

Nation • *Teaching ESL/EFL Reading and Writing*

Nation/Newton • *Teaching ESL/EFL Listening and Speaking*

Kachru/Smith • *Cultures, Contexts, and World Englishes*

McKay/Bokhosrt-Heng • *International English in its Sociolinguistic Contexts: Towards a Socially Sensitive EIL Pedagogy*

Christison/Murray, Eds • *Leadership in English Language Education: Theoretical Foundations and Practical Skills for Changing Times*

McCafferty/Stam, Eds • *Gesture: Second Language Acquisition and Classroom Research*

Liu • *Idioms: Description, Comprehension, Acquisition, and Pedagogy*

Chapelle/Enright/Jamison, Eds • *Building a Validity Argument for the Text of English as a Foreign Language™*

Kondo-Brown/Brown, Eds • *Teaching Chinese, Japanese, and Korean Heritage Students: Curriculum Needs, Materials, and Assessments*

Youmans • *Chicano-Anglo Conversations: Truth, Honesty, and Politeness*

Birch • *English L2 Reading: Getting to the Bottom, Second Edition*

Luk/Lin • *Classroom Interactions as Cross-cultural Encounters: Native Speakers in EFL Lessons*

Levy/Stockwell • *CALL Dimensions: Issues and Options in Computer Assisted Language Learning*

Nero, Ed. • *Dialects, Englishes, Creoles, and Education*

Basturkmen • *Ideas and Options in English for Specific Purposes*

Kumaravadivelu • *Understanding Language Teaching: From Method to Postmethod*

McKay • *Researching Second Language Classrooms*

Egbert/Petrie, Eds • *CALL Research Perspectives*

Canagarajah, Ed. • *Reclaiming the Local in Language Policy and Practice*

Adamson • *Language Minority Students in American Schools: An Education in English*

Fotos/Browne, Eds • *New Perspectives on CALL for Second Language Classrooms*

Hinkel • *Teaching Academic ESL Writing: Practical Techniques in Vocabulary and Grammar*

Hinkel/Fotos, Eds • *New Perspectives on Grammar Teaching in Second Language Classrooms*

Hinkel • *Second Language Writers' Text: Linguistic and Rhetorical Features*

Visit www.routledgeeducation.com for additional information on titles in the ESL & Applied Linguistics Professional Series

Teaching ESL/EFL Listening and Speaking

I. S. P. Nation and J. Newton

Routledge
Taylor & Francis Group

NEW YORK AND LONDON

First published 2009
by Routledge
711 Third Avenue, New York, NY 10017

Simultaneously published in the UK
by Routledge
2 Park Square, Milton Park, Abingdon, Oxon OX14 4RN

Routledge is an imprint of the Taylor & Francis Group, an informa business

© 2009 Routledge, Taylor & Francis

Typeset in Minion by
RefineCatch Limited, Bungay, Suffolk

Library of Congress Cataloging-in-Publication Data
Nation, I. S. P.
    Teaching ESL/EFL listening and speaking / I. S. P. Nation and J. Newton.
        p. cm.—(ESL & applied linguistics professional series)
    Includes bibliographical references and index.
    1. English language—Study and teaching—Foreign speakers. 2. English language—Spoken
English—Study and teaching. 3. Listening—Study and teaching. 4. English teachers—Training
of. I. Newton, J. (Jonathan) II. Title.
    PE1128.A2N344 2008
    2008011763

ISBN10: 0–415–98969–8 (hbk)
ISBN10: 0–415–98970–1 (pbk)
ISBN10: 0–203–89170–8 (ebk)

ISBN13: 978–0–415–98969–5 (hbk)
ISBN13: 978–0–415–98970–1 (pbk)
ISBN13: 978–0–203–89170–4 (ebk)

Printed and bound in Great Britain by
TJ International Ltd, Padstow, Cornwall

Contents

Preface

This book is intended for teachers of English as a second or foreign language. It can be used both for experienced teachers and for teachers in training. In its earlier forms this book has been used on graduate diploma and Masters level courses, and with teachers in training.

The book has two major features. First, it has a strong practical emphasis—around one hundred teaching techniques are described in the book. Second, it tries to provide a balanced programme for developing the skills of listening and speaking. It does this by using a framework called the four strands. These are called strands because they run through the whole course. They are the strands of meaning-focused input, meaning-focused output, language-focused learning, and fluency development. In a well-balanced language programme covering the four skills of listening, speaking, reading, and writing, each of the four strands should have roughly equal amounts of time. The organisation of the book largely reflects these four strands.

We have attempted to write the book using clear and simple language. Wherever possible, technical terms have been avoided. However, in a few cases, with terms such as *negotiation, pushed output,* and *extensive reading,* technical terms have been used and explained in the text. This book thus does not require any previous knowledge of second language acquisition theory or language teaching methodology.

Chapter 1 gives an overview of the four strands. This overview is also very relevant for the companion book to this one, called *Teaching ESL/EFL Reading and Writing.* Chapters 2 and 3 deal largely with listening (a form of meaning-focused input). Chapters 4, 5 and 8 deal with language-focused learning, paying particular attention to dictation and its related activities, and to pronunciation. Chapters 6 and 7 focus on speaking (meaning-focused output). These chapters look at how speaking activities can be designed to encourage language learning. Chapter 9 deals with fluency development, which is the fourth of the strands. Where English is taught as a foreign language, fluency development is often neglected. Fluency development is important at all levels of proficiency, and even beginners need to become fluent with the few items of language that they know. Chapter 10 deals with monitoring and testing.

As a result of working through this book, teachers should be able to design a well-balanced listening and speaking course which provides a good range of opportunities for learning. The teacher's most important job is to plan so that the learners are learning useful things, so that the best conditions for learning occur, and so that they are getting a balance of learning opportunities. This book should help teachers do this.

Wherever possible, the ideas in this book are research based. This is reflected in the principles which are described at the end of Chapter 1 and which are referred to throughout the book. The idea which lies behind these principles is that it is not a wise idea to follow closely a particular method of language teaching, such as communicative language teaching or the direct method. It is much more sensible to draw, where possible, on research-based principles which can be adapted or discarded as new research evidence becomes available.

There are many people who could be thanked for their help in the production of this book. Eli Hinkel gave us a great deal of very supportive encouragement to get us to offer the book for publication. Mary Hillemeier and Naomi Silverman of Taylor & Francis were similarly enthusiastic and took away a lot of the burden of publication. The reviewers of the book before it was published provided many helpful and frank comments which led us to see the book through others' eyes. We are very grateful for this.

Both this book and its companion volume, *Teaching ESL/EFL Reading and Writing*, were largely written and used in our own teacher training courses before they were offered for publication. There was thus a lot of input from the teachers who were studying on these courses.

We would feel that the book's purpose has been achieved, if as a result of reading it, teachers learn some new techniques and activities, understand why these activities are used, and see how they fit into the larger programme.

Teaching English and training teachers of English are challenging but very rewarding professions. We have both been involved in them for a very long time and they have given us a great deal of enjoyment. We hope that this enjoyment is apparent in the book and that it will help readers gain similar enjoyment.

Acknowledgements

Most of Chapter 1 is from an article entitled *The four strands* in the journal *Innovation in Language Teaching and Learning* (2007) 1: 1–12. Parts of Chapter 4 are from an article, *Dictation, dicto-comp and related techniques*, in the journal *English Teaching Forum* (1991) 29, 4: 12–14.

Parts and Goals of a Listening and Speaking Course

This book uses research and theory on second language acquisition in classrooms as the basis for planning a listening and speaking programme for learners of English as a second or foreign language. As we shall see, the principles underlying the listening and speaking parts of a course are not essentially different from those underlying the reading and writing parts.

The Four Strands

The basic argument of the book is that a well-balanced language course should consist of four roughly equal strands:

1. Learning through meaning-focused input; that is, learning through listening and reading where the learner's attention is on the ideas and messages conveyed by the language.
2. Learning through meaning-focused output; that is, learning through speaking and writing where the learner's attention is on conveying ideas and messages to another person.
3. Learning through deliberate attention to language items and language features; that is, learning through direct vocabulary study, through grammar exercises and explanation, through attention to the sounds and spelling of the language, through attention to discourse features, and through the deliberate learning and practice of language learning and language use strategies.
4. Developing fluent use of known language items and features over the

four skills of listening, speaking, reading and writing; that is, becoming fluent with what is already known.

These four strands are called meaning-focused input, meaning-focused output, language-focused learning, and fluency development. A well-planned language course has an appropriate balance of these four strands. It is through these four strands that learners achieve the learning goals of a language course, namely fluent control of the sounds, spelling, vocabulary, grammar and discourse features of the language, so that they can be used to communicate effectively. The opportunities for learning language are called strands because they can be seen as long continuous sets of learning conditions that run through the whole language course. Every activity in a language course fits into one of these strands.

This chapter does not limit itself to listening and speaking, but because it aims at describing what a well-balanced course is like, it also includes the skills of reading and writing. There is a companion text, *Teaching ESL/EFL Reading and Writing*, to this text on listening and speaking.

There is a tendency for language courses not to balance the four strands and indeed to give almost no attention to some of them. Courses which have a very strong communicative focus often actively discourage formal language-focused learning. There is no justification for this as second language acquisition research shows that appropriately focused attention to language items can make a very positive contribution to learning (Doughty, 2003; Doughty and Williams, 1998; Ellis, 2005 and 2006). At the other extreme, there are courses that seem to do little else but focus on formal features of the language with little or no opportunity to use what has been learned to receive and produce real messages. Perhaps even more commonly, there are courses that provide opportunities to receive and produce messages, that give useful attention to language features, but that do not provide opportunities for the learners to become truly fluent in using what they know.

A common-sense justification of the four strands is the time-on-task principle. How can you learn to do something if you don't do that during learning? How can you learn to read if you don't do reading? How can you learn to write without writing? The time-on-task principle simply says that the more time you spend doing something, the better you are likely to be at doing it. This is a very robust principle and there is no shortage of evidence, for example, that those who read a lot are better readers (Cunningham and Stanovich, 1991) and that those who write a lot usually become better writers. However, it is a simplistic principle and it can be rightfully criticised for ignoring the quality of the activity in favour of the quantity of the activity, and for not taking account of the ways in which language learning differs from other kinds of learning. Nevertheless, as one of a set of principles which do take account of these factors, the time-on-task principle is an important and essential one. Another idea underlying a common-sense approach is that there is something about each of the language skills of listening, speaking, reading and writing that makes it different from the others. It is thus necessary to give attention to each skill to make sure that these unique features are learned (DeKeyser, 2007). It is also not difficult to argue that each of these four skills can be broken down even further, for example, that speaking monologue in a formal situation has features that differ from those involved in friendly conversation, and so on (Biber, 1989). It is also possible to distinguish accuracy from fluency and thus see the necessity for providing fluency practice for each of the skills. There are thus common-sense justifications for including the four strands in a language course.

The evidence for the strands draws on a large and growing body of research into the roles of input, output, and form-focused instruction on second language learning, and on the development of speaking and reading fluency. In this chapter we will look at each of the four strands, the research evidence for them, their justification, and how they can be put into practice. The chapter concludes with a set of pedagogical principles based on the strands that can be used to guide the teaching of a language course.

Meaning-focused Input: Learning through Listening and Reading

The meaning-focused input strand involves learning through listening and reading—using language receptively. It is called "meaning-focused" because in all the work done in this strand, the learners' main focus and interest should be on understanding, and gaining knowledge or enjoyment or both from what they listen to and read. Typical activities in this strand include extensive reading, shared reading, listening to stories, watching TV or films, and being a listener in a conversation (see Hinkel, 2006 for a survey of the four skills).

This strand only exists if certain conditions are present:

1. Most of what the learners are listening to or reading is already familiar to them.
2. The learners are interested in the input and want to understand it.
3. Only a small proportion of the language features are unknown to the learners. In terms of vocabulary, 95 percent to 98 percent of the running words should be within the learners' previous knowledge, and so only five or preferably only one or two words per hundred should be unknown to them (Hu and Nation, 2000).

4. The learners can gain some knowledge of the unknown language items through context clues and background knowledge.
5. There are large quantities of input.

If these conditions are not present, then the meaning-focused input strand does not exist in that course. Learning from meaning-focused input is fragile because there are usually only small gains from each meeting with a word, and because learning is dependent on the quality of reading and listening skills, and is affected by background knowledge. Because of this, large quantities of input are needed for this strand to work well. An extensive reading programme is one way of providing this quantity.

Although many researchers criticise Krashen's (1985) input theory, none would disagree with the idea that meaningful comprehensible input is an important source of language learning. Dupuy (1999) investigated "narrow listening", an approach based on Krashen's ideas. This involved learners in listening as many times as they wish to a range of 1–2-minute aural texts on a range of familiar and interesting topics of their choice. The learners in the study reported improvements in their listening comprehension, fluency, and vocabulary, as well as increased confidence in French (the target language). Among the best-controlled studies of second language extensive reading is Waring and Takaki's (2003) study of vocabulary learning from a graded reader. This study showed that small amounts of vocabulary learning of various strengths occurred incidentally as a result of meaning-focused reading. Elley and Mangubhai's (1981) classic study of the book flood (a programme that encouraged wide reading for pleasure) showed a range of language learning benefits compared with a programme that was largely dominated by language-focused learning (or perhaps more accurately, language-focused teaching).

Compared with well-planned deliberate learning, incidental learning through input is fragile and is dependent on large quantities of input to gain sufficient repetition. Nation and Wang (1999) calculated that second language learners needed to read at least one graded reader every two weeks in order to get enough repetitions to establish substantial vocabulary growth through incidental learning. The gains from meaning-focused input, however, become substantial gains if there are large quantities of input.

Meaning-focused Output: Learning through Speaking and Writing

The meaning-focused output strand involves learning through speaking and writing—using language productively. Typical activities in this strand include talking in conversations, giving a speech or lecture, writing a letter, writing a note to someone, keeping a diary, telling a story, and telling someone how to do something.

The same kinds of conditions apply to meaning-focused output as apply to meaning-focused input:

1. The learners write and talk about things that are largely familiar to them.
2. The learners' main goal is to convey their message to someone else.
3. Only a small proportion of the language they need to use is not familiar to them.
4. The learners can use communication strategies, dictionaries, or previous input to make up for gaps in their productive knowledge.
5. There are plenty of opportunities to produce.

Many spoken activities will include a mixture of meaning-focused input and meaning-focused output. One person's output can be another person's input.

Swain's (1985) output hypothesis has been influential in clarifying the role of speaking and writing in second language learning. As its name suggests, the output hypothesis was initially formulated as a reaction to Krashen's (1985) input hypothesis and the inadequacy of the input hypothesis in explaining the effects of immersion education. "Put most simply, the output hypothesis claims that the act of producing language (speaking and writing) constitutes, under certain circumstances, part of the process of second language learning" (Swain, 2005: 471). The opportunities that output provides for learning, however, are not exactly the same as those provided by input. Swain (1995) suggests three functions for output: (1) the noticing/triggering function, (2) the hypothesis testing function, and (3) the metalinguistic (reflective) function.

The noticing/triggering function occurs when learners are attempting to produce the second language and they consciously notice gaps in their knowledge. That is, they do not know how to say what they want to say. Izumi's (2002) research indicates that the effect on acquisition of noticing a gap through output was significantly greater than the effect of noticing through input. This effect can be explained in two ways. First, productive learning involves having to search for and produce a word form, whereas receptive learning involves having to find a meaning for a word form. Productive learning typically results in more and stronger knowledge than receptive learning (Griffin and Harley, 1996). Second, generative use involves meeting or using previously met language items in ways that they have not been used or met before and produces deeper learning than the simple retrieval of previously met items (Joe, 1998). Izumi (2002) suggests that the grammatical encoding that is required by output forces learners to integrate the new items into a more cohesive structure. Decoding items from input does not require this same kind of integration. That is, output sets up learning conditions that are qualitatively different from those of input. This is not to say that input is inferior, simply that it is different and thus an important part of a balanced set of opportunities for learning. The full effect of the noticing/triggering function is not complete until learners have had the chance to make up for the lack that they have noticed. This can occur in several ways. First, having noticed a gap during output, the learners then notice items in input that they did not notice before. If learners notice that there is something they do not know when writing, they later "read like a writer" giving attention to how others say what they wanted to say. This is often referred to as moving from semantic to syntactic processing. This is similar to an amateur guitar player not just enjoying a performance by a top-class guitarist, but also analysing the techniques and chord voicings he or she uses in the hope of copying these later. Second, having noticed a gap during output, learners may success-fully fill that gap through a lucky guess, trial and error, the use of analogy, first language transfer, or problem solving. Webb (2002) found that learn-ers were able to demonstrate aspects of vocabulary knowledge of previ-ously unknown words even though they had not had the opportunity to learn those aspects of knowledge, but which they were able to work out through analogy and first language parallels. Third, having noticed a gap during output, learners may deliberately seek to find the item by reference to outside sources like teachers, peers, or dictionaries.

Swain's second function of output is the hypothesis-testing function. This involves the learner trying out something and then confirming or modifying it on the basis of perceived success and feedback. This hypothesis-testing function is particularly important in interaction when learners negotiate with each other or a teacher to clarify meaning. The feedback provided in negotiation can improve not only the comprehen-sibility of input, but can also be a way for learners to improve their output (Mackey, 2007). Similarly, a large body of research shows that feedback from the teacher during communicative classroom interaction has signifi-cant effects on learning (Leeman, 2007). However, there are many ways of giving feedback and not all are equally effective, a point we discuss in a later chapter. Feedback need not be immediate, as in the case of feedback on writing.

The third function of output is the metalinguistic (reflective) function. This involves largely spoken output being used to solve language problems in collaboration with others. Common classroom applications of this idea include the use of activities like the strip story (Gibson, 1975) and dicto-gloss (Wajnryb, 1988, 1989) where learners work together to construct or reconstruct a text. Similarly, communication tasks called explicit structure-based tasks involve learners in solving grammar problems through meaning-focused output with grammar structures being the topic of communication (Fotos, 2002). All these activities involve a lot of talk about language and this talk can contribute to language learning (Swain and Lapkin, 1998; Swain, 2000). The requirements of such activities are a deliberate reflective focus on language, typically within the context of language in use. Although this is made more likely by interaction, it is not limited to interaction. Other activities encouraging metalinguistic reflection include whiteboard or group composition where learners cooperate to produce one piece of written work and "Ask and Answer" (Simcock, 1993) where learners retell a text in an interview format. These activities combine meaning-focused output and language-focused learning because output becomes the means for deliberately focusing on language features.

It is possible to add a number of additional functions of output. A fourth function involves strengthening knowledge of language items through the way they are used. The most effective use is called "generative use" (Joe, 1998) where the learners use the language items in ways that they have not met or used before. The more generatively something is used, the better it is retained. Additional functions involve developing discourse skills such as turn-taking and skills for dealing with communication problems, developing a personal voice or manner of speaking (Skehan, 1998). These are skills that can only be acquired through active participation in meaning-focused speaking.

Language-focused Learning

Language-focused learning has many names—focus on form, form-focused instruction, deliberate study and deliberate teaching, learning as opposed to acquisition, intentional learning, and so on. It involves the deliberate learning of language features such as pronunciation, spelling, vocabulary, grammar, and discourse. The term language-focused learning is preferred because terms like focus on form and form-focused instruction are misleading in that they can involve a deliberate focus on meaning as well as form, and need not involve instruction but can be the focus of individual autonomous learning. The ultimate aim of language-focused learning is to deal with messages, but its short-term aim is to learn language items. Typical activities in this strand are pronunciation practice, using substitution tables and drills, learning vocabulary from word cards, intensive reading, translation, memorising dialogues, and getting feedback about writing. The deliberate learning of strategies such as guessing from context or dictionary use are also included in this strand. Most of these language-focused learning activities can have a positive effect on learning and language use, but it is important that they are only a small part of the course and do not become the whole course. In total, the language-focused learning strand should not make up more than one-quarter of the time spent on the whole course.

Just as there are conditions for meaning-focused input and output, there are conditions for language-focused learning:

1. The learners give deliberate attention to language features.
2. The learners should process the language features in deep and thoughtful ways.
3. There should be opportunities to give spaced, repeated attention to the same features.
4. The features which are focused on should be simple and not dependent on developmental knowledge that the learners do not have.
5. Features which are studied in the language-focused learning strand should also occur often in the other three strands of the course.

Language-focused learning can have any of these effects:

• it can add directly to implicit knowledge
• it can raise consciousness to help later learning
• it can focus on systematic aspects of the language
• it can be used to develop strategies.

Some activities in the language-focused learning strand, such as dictation, go in and out of fashion, but there is plenty of evidence, certainly in vocabulary learning, that deliberate learning can make a very useful contribution to a learner's language proficiency.

There has long been substantial evidence that deliberately learning vocabulary can result in large amounts of well-retained usable knowledge (Nation, 2001: 296–316). Evidence also shows that very large amounts of learning can occur in limited amounts of learning time, particularly if learning sessions are increasingly spaced. There is evidence that deliberate learning is effective for the learning of multi-word units (Boers, Eyckmans, Kappel, Stengers, and Demecheleer, 2006). Williams (2005) provides a very clear and useful analysis of what might be required for effective deliberate learning of grammatical features (focus on form). There is plenty of evidence that such a focus has positive effects for language learning, but there is debate over whether this has to be within the context of an overall focus on meaning and communication or whether it can be fully decontextualised (Ellis, 2006; Williams, 2005).

Becoming Fluent in Listening, Speaking, Reading and Writing

The fluency development strand should involve all the four skills of listening, speaking, reading and writing. In this strand, the learners are helped to make the best use of what they already know. Like meaning-focused input and output, the fluency development strand is also meaning-focused. That is, the learners' aim is to receive and convey messages. Typical activities include speed reading, skimming and scanning, repeated reading, 4/3/2, repeated retelling, ten-minute writing, and listening to easy stories.

The fluency strand only exists if certain conditions are present.

1. All of what the learners are listening to, reading, speaking or writing is largely familiar to them. That is, there are no unfamiliar language features, or largely unfamiliar content or discourse features.
2. The learners' focus is on receiving or conveying meaning.
3. There is some pressure or encouragement to perform at a faster than usual speed.
4. There is a large amount of input or output.

If the activity involves unknown vocabulary, it is not a fluency activity. If the focus is on language features, it is not a fluency activity. If there is no push to go faster or more smoothly, it is not a fluency activity. The fluency strand should make up about one-quarter of the course time. It is time out from learning new items and is a time for getting good at using what is already known.

Studies of fluency development in first language readers have found that fluency practice increases fluency and that assisted fluency activities seem to work better than unassisted activities (Kuhn and Stahl, 2003). Studies of second language readers have also found an increase in fluency as a result of timed practice (Chung and Nation, 2006), and have found transfer between the first and second languages when language difficulty is controlled for (Bismoko and Nation, 1974; Cramer, 1975; West, 1941). Studies of the 4/3/2 technique, where the same talk is repeated to different listeners in a decreasing time frame (four minutes, then three minutes, then two), have shown increases in fluency during the task, but surprisingly also increases in grammatical accuracy and grammatical complexity (Arevart and Nation, 1991; Nation, 1989a). Schmidt (1992) describes a range of theories to explain fluency development. What is common to many of these is that fluency development involves more formulaic use of larger language chunks or sequences (Wood, 2006). Fluency, accuracy and complexity are most likely interdependent.

There are two major types of second language fluency activities, those that involve repetitive reception or production of the same material as in

4/3/2 and repeated reading, and those that do not as in easy extensive reading or listening. For first language learners, Kuhn and Stahl (2003) found no advantage for one type of fluency practice over the other.

In the early stages of language learning especially, there is value in becoming fluent with a repertoire of useful sentences and phrases such as those listed in Crabbe and Nation's (1991) survival vocabulary. This fits with Palmer's (1925) fundamental guiding principle for the student of conversation—*Memorise perfectly the largest number of common and useful word groups!* Palmer explains that "perfectly" means to a high level of fluency. In most language courses not enough attention is given to fluency development, possibly because it does not involve the learning of new language items and thus is not seen as moving the learners forward in their knowledge of the language.

Balancing the Four Strands

Each strand should have roughly the same amount of time in a well-balanced course which aims to cover both receptive and productive skills. The balancing of time needs to take account of what occurs inside the classroom as well as opportunities for language learning and use outside the classroom.

A teacher can check whether there is a good balance of the strands by noting the language activities that learners are involved in over two weeks or a month, classifying each of these into one or more of the four strands and noting how much time each one took. Ideally each strand should occupy about 25 percent of the course time.

What justification is there for trying to have an equal amount of time for each strand? Ellis (2005) includes the following principles in his list of principles of instructed language learning:

- Instruction needs to ensure that learners focus predominantly on meaning.
- Instruction needs to ensure that learners also focus on form.

The three strands of meaning-focused input, meaning-focused output, and fluency development are meaning-focused strands. They all involve activities where the learners' focus is on communicating and receiving messages. In the meaning-focused input and meaning-focused output strands, this meaning-focused communication pushes the boundaries of learners' knowledge and skill and results in the largely incidental learning of language features. In the fluency development strand, the messages are very easy and familiar ones but they are still the main focus of the activities. Thus three of the four strands, and thus three-quarters of the time, focus predominately on meaning, and one strand, the language-focused learning strand, focuses on form. There is another justification for this three-to-one balance. Given the same amount of time, deliberate language-focused learning activities result in more learning than the incidental learning from meaning-focused activities. For example, the Waring and Takaki (2003) study showed that in approximately 56 minutes of meaning-focused reading of a graded reader, four words were learned reasonably well, and another 12 were partially learned. Studies of deliberate vocabulary learning when learners study word pairs (2L–1L) result in learning rates of around 35 words per hour which are four or more times higher than the incidental rate (Nation, 2001: 298; Thorndike, 1908; Webb, 1962). This kind of comparison is not entirely fair, however, because meaning-focused activities have a range of benefits for language learning, gaining content matter knowledge, skill improvement and enjoyment. Nonetheless, a major justification for language-focused learning is its focused efficiency. This focused efficiency needs to be balanced against the three less efficient but more widely beneficial meaning-focused strands.

In spite of these arguments, giving equal time to each strand is an arbitrary decision. It has been suggested that the time given to the strands could change as learners' proficiency develops (Ellis, 2002). At the beginning stages there could be more language-focused learning and less fluency development. At the higher proficiency levels, fluency development could take a greater proportion of the time. We are not in favour of this as there are good arguments for developing fluency with items like numbers and useful multi-word phrases right from the beginning of language learning. Similarly, learning more about the nature of language such as its history, etymology and pragmatic effects can be a useful support for learning at advanced levels.

Integrating the Four Strands

The four strands are opportunities for certain types of learning. They differ from each other according to the conditions which are needed for the different types of learning. They can fit together in many different ways. For example, in an intensive English programme with many different teachers, there may be different classes for spoken language (listening and speaking), reading, writing and language study. It would then be important to make sure that the spoken language classes, for example, not only had meaning-focused input and output activities, but also included fluency development activities and only a very small amount of language-focused learning.

In a content-based course which did not have a skill-based division of classes, the four strands could all occur within a unit of work. Language-focused learning could lead into meaning-focused input or output, and this could lead into a fluency activity on the same theme. Alternatively, language-focused learning could occur as it was needed in the context of meaning-focused work. Once again, a good teacher would be quickly checking to see if over a week or two there was a roughly equal amount of time given to each strand.

There are many ways of giving time to the four strands and these will depend on many factors like the skills and preferences of the teachers, the expectations of learners and the school, the time-tabling constraints, and current beliefs about language teaching and learning. What is important is that over a period of time, each strand gets about the same amount of time.

Principles and the Four Strands

The following pedagogical principles are aimed at providing guidelines for teachers. They draw on an earlier larger list (Nation, 1993) and can usefully be compared with other lists of principles (Brown, 1993; Ellis, 2005; Krahnke and Christison, 1983). The list is organised around the four strands with the final two principles focusing on what should be covered in a course. Each principle is followed by a brief list of suggestions about how the principle could be put into practice.

1. *Provide and organise large amounts of comprehensible input through both listening and reading.* This could involve providing an extensive reading programme, reading to the learners, getting learners to give talks for their classmates to listen to, arranging spoken communication activities, and interaction via the internet.

2. *Boost learning through comprehensible input by adding a deliberate element.* Note words on the board as they occur in listening, do consciousness-raising activities before communicative tasks, get learners to reflect on new items they meet while reading, explain problem items that come up in the context of communication activities.

3. *Support and push learners to produce spoken and written output in a variety of appropriate genres.* Use communication activities in a range of situations, use role plays, match writing and speaking tasks to learner needs.

4. *Provide opportunities for cooperative interaction.* Do group work involving opinion gap and information gap tasks, get learners to work together on writing and reading.

5. *Help learners deliberately learn language items and patterns, including*

sounds, spelling, vocabulary, multi-word units, grammar, and discourse. Do teacher-led intensive reading, give feedback on writing, deliberately teach language items, arrange individual study of language items.

6. *Train learners in strategies that will contribute to language learning.* Work on guessing from context, dictionary use, word part analysis, and learning using word cards.

7. *Provide fluency development activities in each of the four skills of listening, speaking, reading and writing.* Run a speed reading course, include repeated reading, provide an extensive reading programme, do 4/3/2 activities, organise a regular ten-minute writing programme, do listening to stories.

8. *Provide a roughly equal balance of the four strands of meaning-focused input, meaning-focused output, language-focused learning, and fluency development.* Keep a record of the activities done in the course, the strand they fit into, and the amount of time spent on them.

9. *Plan for the repeated coverage of the most useful language items.* Focus on high frequency items, use controlled and simplified material, provide plenty of input at the same level.

10. *Use analysis, monitoring and assessment to help address learners' language and communication needs.*

The main aim of this book is to show the wide range of activities that can be used in each of the four strands of a course, to show the research evidence that justifies the existence of the strands, and to show how teachers can monitor and assess the learning that occurs in each of the strands.

A basic assumption that lies behind the book is that it is not wise for a teacher or course designer to ally themselves with a particular method of language teaching. It is much more productive to become aware of the important principles of teaching and learning and to apply these in ways that suit the learners, the teaching conditions and the skills of the teacher. This may result in courses that use different kinds of teaching and learning activities but which fundamentally draw on the same principles.

Another related assumption behind this book is that teaching and learning activities that have become unfashionable for a variety of reasons may still make a positive contribution to learning if they apply useful principles and if they are focused on worthwhile goals. Thus, in this book there is considerable discussion of pronunciation practice, structure drills, learning words out of context, dictation activities and repetition activities. This is because each of these activities, performed in an appropriate way, can contribute to one of the strands of a course. The trick lies in giving them a useful focus and a suitable amount of time.

This book is written for teachers of English as a second or foreign language and, as a result of working their way through it, they should be able to do the following things:

1. Recognise and describe the range of goals of a language course.
2. Look critically at a language course to see its strengths, weaknesses and gaps.
3. Develop and adapt courses to provide a balance of the four strands in a course.
4. Choose, apply and monitor a range of activities that will reach useful learning goals.
5. Be able to describe and justify the parts of their language course drawing on principles derived from research in second language learning and second language teaching.

In each section of this book there will be discussion of how much time in a course should be given to each of the four strands and the sub-strands within them. Teachers will need to look at opportunities for learning outside class and consider these when planning a course.

Learning Goals

A language learning course is used to reach learning goals. These goals can include the learning of: (1) language items such as sounds, vocabulary and grammatical constructions, (2) the content or ideas of the subject being studied such as geography, English literature, mathematics, or cross-cultural understanding, (3) language skills such as listening, writing, fluency in using known items, and strategies for coping with language difficulties, and (4) the organisation of discourse such as rhetorical features and communication strategies. Table 1.1 elaborates these areas. The mnemonic **LIST**, which contains the first letter of each of the goals, is a useful way to remember the goals.

A more detailed elaboration of some of these areas can be found in Munby's (1978: 176–184) taxonomy of language skills.

The use of particular language teaching techniques is justified to the extent that they achieve learning goals. This even applies to techniques that are used for fun to give the learners a break, because there are many language teaching techniques that are great fun and achieve very useful learning goals.

The separate listing of specific goals like pronunciation, vocabulary, and fluency does not mean that there must be a discrete point approach to

Table 1.1 Learning Goals

General goals	Specific goals
Language items	pronunciation
	vocabulary
	grammatical constructions
Ideas (content)	
Skills	listening, speaking, reading, and writing skills or subskills
	accuracy
	fluency
	strategies
Text (discourse)	conversational discourse patterns and rules
	text schemata or topic type scales

teaching. The purpose of such a listing is to make teachers more analytical about their use of techniques and the design of programmes. As we shall see, one technique can achieve several goals and at times it may not be obvious to the learners what the goal is as their interest may be on the message involved in the activity.

Some books describe the skill components and the nature of listening and speaking (Rost, 2002; Thornbury, 2005). Such descriptions give a teacher more realistic expectations of what may be achieved in a course and what to look for to see if the range of knowledge and skills is being covered. Such descriptions also play a role in sequencing the sub-goals of a course.

The text or discourse goals are clearly related to language goals. Biber's research (1989) has shown that various grammatical aspects of the language tend to form different clusters according to the type of discourse. Biber set up a typology of texts based on the co-occurrence of language features. He found that he was able to group texts according to the language features that frequently occurred or which were typically absent or infrequent. For example, face-to-face interaction is typified by the use of time and place adverbials, first- and second-person pronouns, the present tense, private verbs like *know* and *think*, and *be* as a main verb. Imaginative narrative is typified by past tense verbs, third-person pronouns, public verbs like *said*, and present participial clauses.

Biber's findings are important for designing courses, because we can draw the following implications from them.

1. In order to meet the full range of language features, learners need to be exposed to a range of discourse types.
2. Being able to operate well in one kind of discourse, for example informal conversation, does not mean that a learner has the knowledge to operate well in another kind of discourse, for example formal speech, because each discourse type makes use of a different cluster of language features.
3. Having to operate in an unfamiliar discourse area is a demanding task for learners and may make them aware of gaps in their command of the language. As Ellis (1990) points out, this awareness is a prerequisite to language acquisition.

We have looked at the broad features that should make up a well-balanced language course. In the following chapters we will look in detail at what should make up a well-balanced listening and speaking course. The following chapters are based on the idea of the four strands and look at what can make up each strand.

CHAPTER 2

Beginning to Listen and Speak in Another Language

The aims of a beginners course in listening and speaking are: (1) to help the learners to be able to cope with meaning-focused input and meaning-focused output as soon as possible; (2) to motivate them in their language study by getting them to engage in successful listening and speaking; and (3) to make the early learning as relevant as possible to their language use needs.

What Should They Learn?

The content of an English course for beginners will vary greatly according to the age of the learners, their purpose for learning, their educational background and previous experience with English, and whether they are learning in a foreign or second language context. Below is a set of learning priorities for one type of beginners, namely new migrant adult absolute beginners who may have had limited education and who need general everyday English for living in an English-speaking context.

1. *Using a New Alphabet*
   - Recognise and write the letters of the alphabet (including upper and lower case letters). This could involve lots of copying tasks
   - Develop phonological awareness, that letters in words stand for specific sounds, including vowel consonant patterns, three letter words (consonant—vowel—consonant), consonant blends, etc.

2. *Phrases for Talking about Yourself*
   - My name is _____. I live in _____. I come from _____.
   - I am _____ years old. I am married. I have _____ children.
   - I worked as a _____.
   - I like _____. I don't like _____.

3. *Phrases and Vocabulary for Everyday Life*
   - Shopping—food, clothing names, household objects
   - Visiting the doctor
   - Housing
   - Using the telephone
   - Banking
   - Finding a job
   - Contacting government agencies

4. *Sight Vocabulary*
   - Reading street signs, tickets, labels, etc.

5. *Classroom Expressions*
   - Excuse me . . .
   - Say that again please?
   - How do I say this?
   - Can you help me?
   - How do you spell _____?
   - I don't know. I don't understand.
   - Please speak more slowly.
   - May I go to the toilet?

6. *High Frequency Words*
   - Numbers
   - Classroom objects
   - Colours
   - Time and date words
   - Family members
   - Parts of the body
   - Objects in the home
   - Simple question forms

If the learners are adults who wish to use the language while travelling, then learning the survival vocabulary (Appendix 1) is a sensible early goal. This collection of around 120 sentences and phrases has been designed to be immediately useful and to fill the needs of getting to places, finding food and accommodation, being polite, shopping, and getting help.

If the learners are children, then they should learn the high frequency words of the language which allow them to listen to simple stories, begin to read graded readers, and do interesting activities.

Where possible the course should try to address the learners' language needs and should do this so that the learners can see that this is being done. In small classes this can involve the use of a negotiated syllabus (Clarke, 1991) where the teacher and learners work together to decide what will be dealt with in class.

How Should the Teaching and Learning be Done?

Five Principles for Teaching Beginners

One way to answer this question is through a set of principles. Here are five principles that are particularly relevant to the teaching of beginners:

1	Meaning	Focus on meaningful and relevant language
2	Interest	Maintain interest through a variety of activities
3	New language	Avoid overloading learners with too much new language
4	Understanding	Provide plenty of comprehensible input
5	Stress-free	Create a friendly, safe, cooperative classroom environment

Notice that the first letter for each of the key words spells out the acronym "MINUS". This provides a useful aid for remembering the principles. We now discuss the principles in relation to the teaching of absolute beginners in an ESL context. This is, of course, only one of many contexts for teaching beginners, and so readers will need to consider its relevance to their particular teaching context, and how the examples can be adapted to suit this context.

Principle 1. Focus on Meaningful and Relevant Content

The main focus should be on language that the learners can use quickly for their purposes rather than on too much grammar explanation or on words that are not directly useful. Here are some simple sentences that can be learnt very early in a course so that the learners can use them straight away:

My name is _____.
I come from _____.
I live in _____.
My address is _____.

The teacher could present these sentences orally, one by one, with gestures and lots of repetition and learner involvement. The sentences could then be written on a whiteboard so that the learners can write them down. The written versions then become the basis for pair work. The first aim of this learning is for learners to be able to say these things about themselves without looking at the written version, and to understand other learners when they use them. The second aim is for learners to begin to link the written and spoken forms of the words. For learners who are not very familiar with the written form of English, recognising the written form of their name and address is an important early step in building literacy.

One way of checking the usefulness of a phrase or word is to use a computer concordancer to see how many examples of the item can be found in a collection of spoken texts. A useful starting point is http://www.lextutor.ca/concordancers/.

One of the most useful techniques in a listening and speaking programme is the teacher engaging in meaning-focused dialogue with the learners. This dialogue can have many different focuses.

1. *Classroom management.* Perhaps the most realistic kind of dialogue involves the day-to-day running of the classroom. This includes: (1) organising classroom work such as forming groups, using the course book, and calling on learners to perform tasks; (2) keeping control of noise and behaviour; (3) checking attendance; and (4) thanking and praising.
2. *Informal conversation.* The teacher and learners talk about things that happened outside school. Where appropriate this can be about the learner's family, their hobbies, how they travel to school, favourite food, and so on.
3. *Recalling previous lessons.* The teacher and learners talk about previous class work. This draws on what is hopefully known and familiar and also provides opportunities for revision.
4. *Finding out learners' opinions and ideas.* During an activity the teacher can ask the learners if they like the particular activity and if they want to do more of it. This dialogue can be the early beginnings of a partly negotiated syllabus.

Principle 2. Maintain Interest Through a Variety of Activities

To maintain learners' interest, activities need to be short and varied, and to involve the learners in responding to or using the language. Here are some simple ways to keep learners interested in learning:

- do activities that involve movement
- use real objects and pictures

- plan trips outside the classroom, for example, a trip to a local supermarket linked to a simple food search game
- use songs and simple chants in between other more demanding activities
- introduce and practise new content though games such as bingo.

Principle 3. Avoid Overloading Learners with Too Much New Language

There is usually little need to focus on grammar in the early parts of a course for beginners. Instead lessons should focus on learning set phrases and words. Teachers often make the mistake of introducing too much new language without giving learners enough opportunities to gain control over this language. A simple rule to keep in mind is *"learn a little, use a lot"*. For example, if the goal is to learn the names for parts of the body, it is better to focus on the most useful words such as *head, neck, arms, hands, legs, feet,* and so on, and to avoid less common words such as *elbow* and *ankle*. Note that introducing *elbow* and *ankle* at the same time creates another problem; the similarities between these words (i.e., they sound a bit the same and their meanings are related) is likely to lead to learners confusing each word for the other.

To apply the principle of *"learn a little, use a lot"*, the body words need to be practised in a variety of ways. These could include picture games, information transfer activities, action games ("Simon says . . ."), and bingo. The words can then be used in simple sentence patterns and dialogues such as *"How are you? Not so good. My _____ hurts"*. These activities are described later in this chapter.

Principle 4. Provide Plenty of Comprehensible Input

Note that most of these activities mentioned above first involve learners in learning the words through listening and doing before they deepen their learning through using the words in guided speaking. If speaking is pushed too early, learners may be more likely to transfer L1 phonology and to concentrate on mechanical difficulties. Activities like listen and do, picture ordering, bingo and information transfer show how listening can be practised in very active ways without requiring much speaking.

To ensure that input can be understood requires the use of visual aids and contextual support for new language including pictures, gestures, mime, objects, and experiences out of class. Teachers also need to think carefully about the language they use in class with the aim of keeping their talk simple but not simplistic or ungrammatical. One way to do this is to always use one form for one meaning. Thus, for example, the teacher needs to decide whether to use "My name is _____" or "I am

_____ ", but not both; "Where are you from?" or "Where do you come from?", but not both.

Early in the course learners can also learn simple phrases for controlling input such as, "*Sorry, I don't understand*", "*Please say it again*". Displaying these phrases on a large poster makes them readily available throughout a course.

Most of these ideas assume a context in which learners speak a variety of first languages, or the teacher does not speak the learners' first language. Of course, teaching beginners is easier if the learners all speak the same first language and the teacher speaks the first language of the learners. Using translation to convey the meanings of words and phrases is very efficient and is well supported by research as an effective way of communicating meaning. The main disadvantage is that the teacher and learners are tempted to use a lot of classroom time using the first language instead of the second language. However, as long as the teacher is aware of this danger, then using the first language is a good thing to do and saves a lot of time.

If the learners do not all speak the same first language, and if the teacher does not speak the first languages of the learners, then pictures, gestures and the use of context need to be used to get meaning across. This is not as difficult as it sounds, and if the learners also have a well-illustrated course book, the job is easier.

Older learners may make use of bilingual dictionaries which give the meanings of second language words in the learners' first language. These dictionaries differ a lot in quality, but they are extremely useful learning aids. Learners need to have a second language vocabulary of at least 2000 words before they can use monolingual dictionaries where meanings are given in the second language. This is because a vocabulary of around 2000 words is needed to write and understand definitions.

Principle 5. Create a Friendly, Safe, Cooperative Classroom Environment

There is strong evidence that anxiety influences learners' willingness to communicate in a second language (e.g., Yashima, 2002). Therefore, it is particularly important that, in the early stages of learning a second language, learners have successful, low stress learning experiences. By paying attention to the first four principles, there is a very good chance that these experiences will be plentiful, and that the teacher will already be meeting this fifth principle. Some of the factors that contribute to a positive beginners' classroom are variety, movement, physical comfort, frequent interaction, successful language experiences, and opportunities for learners to experiment and make mistakes without penalties.

Activities and Approaches for Teaching and Learning in a Beginners' Course

Memorising Useful Phrases and Sentences

A quick way of gaining early fluency in a language is to memorise useful phrases. There are several advantages in doing this. First, simple communication can occur at an early stage. For example, learners should be able to say who they are, where they come from, and what they do from the very first language lessons. They should also be able to greet people with phrases like *good morning*, and *good day* and to thank them. Second, memorising phrases and sentences allows learners to make accurate use of the language without having to know the grammar. Third, as we have seen, knowing sentences like *Please say that again, Please speak more slowly, What does X mean?* allows learners to take control of a conversation and use it for language learning purposes. Fourth, the words and patterns that make up such phrases can make the learning of later phrases and perhaps the learning of later patterns easier. Even at this very early stage of language learning, it is worth showing learners the value of making small cards with the second language word or phrase on one side and the first language translation on the other. These cards are used for recalling the meanings of the words and phrases, and later recalling the words and phrases. The learner carries a pack of these cards around and goes through them when they have a free moment. Research has shown that this spaced recall is a very effective way of learning (Nation, 2001: 296–316), and results in the kind of knowledge needed for normal language use.

There are several ways of deciding what sentences and phrases to learn. The following list is ranked in order of importance.

1. The learners think of things they want to be able to say and the teacher provides the second language phrase to say this.
2. The teacher thinks of the uses the learners need to make of the language and thinks of useful phrases to meet these needs. In some cases this may involve the teacher talking to the learners about their language needs and observing their daily use of the language.
3. The teacher consults lists of useful and frequent phrases that researchers have developed.
4. The teacher follows a course book.

Here is an example of what can happen if not much thought is given to what is taught. Gareth is in his fifth month of learning Japanese in the first year of secondary school. He is speaking to a researcher.

"Tell me something in Japanese, Gareth."
"OK. You ask me questions in English and I'll answer in Japanese."

"Were you born in New Zealand?"
"We haven't got up to 'yes' yet."
"All right. I'll try something else. How old are you?"
"Do you want me to say the whole sentence because I can only say the number?"
"That's fine. Just tell me the number."
". . . . ."
"That sounds good. Here's another question. What do you do at school?"
"No, not that kind of thing."
"Sorry. What sort of thing should I be asking you?"
"Well all the regular things like 'This is a pen' and 'The book is red'. That kind of thing."

Practising Sentence Patterns

The next step from memorising phrases and sentences is to learn some productive sentence patterns, that is, sentences where regular substitutions can be made to produce other sentences. These are called **substitution tables**. Here is an example.

1	2	3	4	5
I	'll	see	you	tomorrow.
		meet		on Friday.
		call		next week.
				at six o'clock.

The sentence has five parts, but in the example, substitutions are only made in two of them. When the pattern is first introduced, it is best to have substitution only in one part. The first step is to memorise one sentence, *I'll see you tomorrow.* Then the teacher gets the learners to take turns around the class making a systematic substitution in one part, for example *tomorrow, on Friday*, etc. The teacher should give the learner an oral cue before they make the substitution.

Teacher:	I'll see you tomorrow. On Friday.
Learner 1:	I'll see you on Friday.
Teacher:	next week
Learner 2	I'll see you next week.
Teacher:	at six o'clock
Learner 3:	I'll see you at six o'clock.

When a new pattern or substitution table is introduced the teacher should start regularly. That is, the teacher should go through the table so that the learners can tell what the next sentence will be, and who will have to say it.

		eating ice-cream
		playing football
	hate	going to the cinema
I	like	studying geography
	love	walking in the evening
		reading comics

For example, when the teacher introduces this substitution table, it can start in a regular way with the teacher saying "I hate eating ice-cream" and then pointing to *playing football.* The first learner in the first row says "I hate playing football". Then the teacher points to *going to the cinema* and the second learner in the first row says the new sentence and so on.

> T: I hate eating ice-cream. (points to *playing football*)
> L1: I hate playing football.
> T: (points to *going to the cinema*)
> L2: I hate going to the cinema.

When this is easy for the learners the teacher can point to phrases in any order. When this is easy for the learners, the teacher points to a phrase and then points to any learner with the other hand. Thus, the learners do not know what phrase will be next and who will be the next person to speak. So the teacher keeps the exercise interesting by increasing the amount of irregularity in the use of the table (George, 1965).

Another way to keep the exercise interesting is for the teacher to increase the speed of pointing at the table or at the learners. The learners thus have less time to think. The teacher should be careful that the learners do not say the sentences too quickly because of this.

Another way to keep the exercise interesting is to make the learners use their memory. If the table is written on the board, the teacher can gradually rub out words and phrases. The teacher still points to the whiteboard but often points to an empty space and the learners must remember what was there in order to say the sentence. To make it easier, when the words are rubbed out, they can be replaced by drawings or words in the first language. Or, after the learners have used a substitution table for a short time, it is rubbed off the whiteboard or the learners close their books. Then the teacher says parts of phrases and the learners must say the whole sentence. So, using the above substitution table the teacher would say, "I hate eating ice-cream playing." The learners must remember that *playing* was followed by *football* in the table and so the learner says, "I hate playing football." Then the teacher says "comics" and so on.

There is a danger in the use of substitution tables. The items which are listed in one column, *on Friday, next week, at six o'clock,* tend to be related in meaning and so can interfere with each other. Thus learners may later incorrectly recall items like *on next week, at Friday*. The teacher should plan substitutions with this possibility in mind (for example, don't include *on Friday*), and should look to see if interference is occurring.

So far we have looked at a range of language-focused activities to use in the beginning stages of a language course involving memorising phrases and sentences, and practising sentence patterns. These are all useful short-cuts to getting started in a language, but do not directly develop the implicit knowledge needed for normal language use. The following activities move closer to meaning-focused input and meaning-focused output where the focus is on communicating messages. Although many techniques are described below, the teacher should choose a few of these to use regularly. This helps set up known, predictable routines which make class-room management easier and allow the focus to be on the communication rather than on managing the activity. Other activities can be brought in occasionally for variety.

Guiding Listening and Speaking

The prototypical technique for guided listening and speaking is the **What is it?** technique (Nation, 1978).

The teacher writes some sentences on the blackboard. The sentences describe something or someone. Here is an example:

It is <u>thin</u>.
It is <u>black</u>.
It has <u>many teeth</u>.
It is made of <u>plastic</u>.
We can find it <u>near a mirror</u>.
It costs <u>a dollar</u>.
<u>Everybody</u> uses it.
It is used for <u>combing your hair</u>.
What is it?

The teacher shows the learners how to change the sentences to talk about different things. While she does this the teacher follows the plan very closely. For example, *a needle*:

It is thin.
It is silver.
It has a sharp point.
It is made of steel.
We can find it in our house.
It costs ten cents.

You need good eyes to use it.
It is used for sewing things.
What is it?

Then the teacher gives the learners the name of something, for example, *a pen* and they must describe it using the plan. She gives a few new words if they are needed in the description. Each learner can be given a different item written on a card to describe. When the learners know how to follow the plan, it can be played as a game. One learner describes something while the others try to guess what it is. As they improve, the learners can add some sentences that are not in the plan and make other changes. The exercise can be made more controlled by asking the learners to follow the sentence patterns of the plan very carefully.

This technique has the following features:

1. Learners can be prepared for the activity by learning and practising a small number of sentence patterns.
2. Communication is important because the activity has an outcome that depends on successful communication.
3. The learners can do the activity with each other in a form of pair and group work. In this way the activity provides opportunities for both listening and speaking to occur.
4. Learners can make changes to the activity so that the outcome is not completely predictable.

The following activity has the same features. **Listening grids** (Badger, 1986) involve using listening and often questioning to fill a matrix with information. Here is an example based on what people enjoy watching on television. Each learner makes a short presentation describing what they like, using the construction "I enjoy watching . . .". The rest of the group tick the appropriate places in their grids.

Table 2.1 Listening Grids

Person's name	News	Comedy	Game shows	Adventure

It is only a small step from grids to **surveys**. Each learner has a grid or a list of questions which are then used to gather information from other learners in the class. This can be done with each learner moving around the class. Surveys may also move out of the classroom to involve English speakers at home or at work, or learners in another class.

Table 2.2 Surveys

(a) *Family*

What's your name?	Have you got any brothers?	Have you got any sisters?	Have you got any children?

(b) *Things*

What's your name?	Have you got:			
	a car	a bicycle	a cat	a television

Interview activities provide small-scale question and answer interaction. The activities using grids and surveys described above can easily become like small interviews. The person being interviewed needs a source of knowledge, for example personal experience, a report from a newspaper, part of a science, mathematics or economics textbook, a picture or a brief written description. The interviewer needs some guidance on what information to look for and what kinds of questions to ask. If, for example, several learners or pairs of learners have a different car advertisement each, then they can be interviewed several times by different learners who are using a standard set of questions or the same grid to fill in.

Quizzes are often simply listening activities with an element of competition. The teacher prepares general knowledge questions, incomplete statements, or true/false statements that the learners will hear and try to answer. There may be two competing teams with an audience who also write their own answers to the questions. It is not difficult to design quiz questions around a few grammatical constructions.

The airline of Belgium is called _____.
The long thin parts of a comb are called _____.

An element of challenge or competition is also present in **puzzles**. Puzzles may be based on pictures or brief descriptions and give meaning-focused practice in listening.

the hill

the farm ························· the city

the sea

A boy faces the city.	A girl faces the farm.
What is on his right side?	Where is the hill?
What is behind him?	What is on her left side?

Puzzles based on pictures can involve the use of inference. For example, the learners may have to decide what season it is, what the weather is like on that day in the picture, how old the people are, and so on.

Listen and do activities are used in most classrooms and are the basis of Total Physical Response language teaching (Asher, Kosudo and de la Torre, 1974). In these activities the teacher gives commands or makes statements and the learners do what the teacher says. There are many possible variations on these activities. They can become speaking activities with the learners saying what to do and the teacher or another learner doing the action. In **positioning**, some of the learners see a photograph or picture and have to tell other learners how to position themselves to appear like the people in the picture. This can also include the expressions on their faces (Hughes, 1985). Blindfolded learners may be guided through a series of minor obstacles by following the spoken instructions of others.

Bingo is a very adaptable activity that provides learners with lots of listening and vocabulary practice. In "body part bingo" (McKay and Tom, 1999) the teacher first reads simple descriptions of main body parts and learners guess what is being referred to. Learners then draw a grid with the required number of boxes (3 × 3, 5 × 5, etc.) for the number of body parts. The teacher dictates the names of the body parts and the learners fill in the grid in any order with these names. The game begins with the teacher reading out descriptions of body parts in random order and the learners covering the matching words. The first learner to cover a row in any direction calls out "body". He or she then reads back the covered words.

The **listening to pictures** technique (McComish, 1982) is an excellent example of a technique that involves a large quantity of material to listen to, and which uses a supporting picture to make the language input comprehensible. The learners have a big picture in front of them in which several things are happening. The teacher starts describing the picture, and the learners follow the description while looking at the picture. Occasionally the teacher includes a true/false statement. If the description is recorded, this can be preceded by a buzz to warn learners that the next statement is a test. The learners write T or F on a sheet of paper, the correct answer is given, and the description continues. Some important features of this technique are that it is very easy to prepare and to mark, and the same picture can be used several times if different descriptions are used with it. The teacher moves systematically and predictably through the picture, describing it. For example, the description may start in the top left corner and move across. This means the learners have little difficulty in following the movement and matching the parts of the picture to the spoken input.

Information transfer activities can be used to help learners produce a description involving several sentences (Palmer, 1982). For example, the information transfer diagram could consist of small pictures and phrases showing the process of cooking a certain food, or making something such as a clay pot. Most of the sentences needed in the description would be in the passive (White, 1978). The learner could repeat the description several times, each time with a different audience and with less opportunity to consult the information transfer diagram.

Techniques for Early Meaning-focused Speaking

The following techniques allow learners to produce spoken language mainly in single sentence turns. The first techniques listed below are directed towards question making. The learners' focus will be largely on the meaning as there is usually a game-like element of guessing or competition in the activities. As most of the techniques involve learners making the same kinds of sentences around the group, there is the chance for learners to notice what others do and use it to improve their own performance. The design features of modelled repetitive turn-taking, mixed proficiency groups, and productive tasks thus make it possible for learning through comprehending, noticing, comparing, and using to occur.

Descriptions involve the learners making statements based on pictures. The statements may be descriptions, comparisons, predictions, pointing out the differences between two pictures, explanations of what happened before the event shown in the picture, and so on. The learners can take turns producing a sentence each around the group, or can call on each other.

Duppenthaler (1988) suggests an interesting variation of "What is it?" called **Hints**. The learners are divided into groups of four or five. Each group thinks of a word in their first language, such as the name of a national dish. The group then prepares one sentence for each learner in the group that describes the word. Then the learners say the sentences and points are awarded to the group that guesses it. If after all the sentences are said, it still cannot be guessed then the team who made the sentences loses points.

Learners often need practice in making questions. Gurrey (1955) divides questions into three types—**stage one, two and three questions**. Stage one questions ask for an answer that can be pointed to either in a picture or a reading passage, for example, "What is behind the house?", "Who did John meet?" Stage two questions make the learners think. The answer to a stage two question is not directly stated in the passage or cannot be pointed to in a picture. The learners must put certain facts together to find the answer. After a learner answers a stage two question, the teacher can usually ask "How do you know this?" Here are some stage two questions that are based on a picture. "What season is it?" "What country do these people come from?" To answer these questions the learners must put certain facts together to find the answers. Stage three questions ask learners to use their imagination, for example, "What are these people thinking about?" "Why does this person like wearing blue clothes?" The questions cannot be answered by looking at a picture or a reading passage. Learners can move through these stages of questions while asking each other questions about an event, a picture, or a story.

The learners are divided into tourists and information officers for the **ask and move** activity (Buckeridge, 1988). Each tourist has a different card telling the tourist to find out four or five pieces of information, such as, "Find out the address of the Automobile Association". The information officers have the answers to these requests but each information officer does not have all the information. So, it is necessary for each tourist to go to several information officers to find out all the answers. This will involve the information officers answering the same questions several times.

Twenty questions is a well-known activity. The teacher or a learner thinks of an object and writes its name on a piece of paper. The learners ask yes/no questions, for example, "Is it in the room?", "Is it big?" They must guess what it is before they have asked 20 questions. The person who guesses correctly thinks of the next object and the other learners ask questions.

Questions that are not grammatically correct should not be answered. In another game, a learner can pretend to have a certain job or to be a famous person. The others ask them questions to try to guess their job or who they are. In this game pronominal questions can be used. Instead of thinking of an object the teacher can show an unfamiliar object to the class and by asking yes/no questions, the learners find out what it is.

In **walk and talk**, the learners form two circles with a person in the inner circle being paired with a person in the outer circle. The person in the inner circle tells their partner what they did during the weekend. Then they move two persons to the right and tell their new partner. Later in the whole class a few learners tell what one of their partners told them.

The learners work in pairs for **the same or different** activity. They each have a sheet of numbered sentences and words. They do not show their sheets to each other. The one with the cross next to number 1 begins speaking. The learner with the sentence says it and the other learner provides the word. They decide if the sentence and the word refer to the same thing or different things.

Learner A		Learner B	
1x	It usually has four legs.	1	a chair
2	a boat	2x	It flies through the air.
3x	It has one eye.	3	a needle
4	a book	4x	We can read it.

In another version, the learners decide if the word and the sentence describe the same thing or different things. Instead of words and sentences, only sentences can be used. The learners decide if the two sentences have almost the same meaning or quite different meanings.

Learner A		Learner B	
1x	A car costs a lot of money.	1	A car is expensive.
2	I agree with you.	2x	You and I have the same idea about this.
3x	I failed to meet him.	3	We met only once.

The learners are given sets of four words and have to decide which word is the **odd one out**, that is, it does not belong in the set (Burton, 1986). For example, a set can be

grammar based: *sung, broken, drank, rung;*
vocabulary based: *hand, heart, leg, ear;*
or content based: *Delhi, Jakarta, Hanoi, Berlin.*

The learners describe why the word chosen is the odd one out.

All the activities described in this chapter involve group work where the learners interact with each other using very limited English. It is always useful for the teacher to model the activity for the learners before they get involved in their groups.

A Note on Pronunciation

The older the learners, the more important it is to give some direct attention to pronunciation in the beginning stages of language learning. Pronunciation difficulties for most learners are the result of differences between the sound system of their first language and the sound system of the second language. Adults are less likely to pick up the new sounds than young children. (We will look at the reasons for this in a later chapter.) Giving early attention to difficult sounds like the beginning of *the* and the beginning of *ship* can be helpful in developing an accurate pronunciation. This practice can involve listening to the sounds, distinguishing the sounds, copying the teacher making the sound in easy syllables (consonant plus vowel), looking at the teacher's mouth to see the position of the tongue, teeth and lips, and getting some simple explanation and feedback from the teacher. This directed attention should only take up a small part of each lesson. Its greatest value is in making the learners aware of the differences between the first and second languages. Pronunciation is looked at in detail in Chapter 5.

Planning a Listening and Speaking Programme for Beginners

There should be regular opportunities for increasing amounts of meaning-focused listening input early in a language course. When planning for this it is worth making a distinction between just listening to input, **listen and enjoy**, and the various other listening techniques described in this chapter and elsewhere which require some visible response from the learners, such as **listen and draw, What is it?, listening to pictures**, and **information transfer**.

Listen and enjoy can have its regular daily or weekly time when the learners listen to the continuation of an interesting story in much the same way as people follow a television serial.

If there is no opportunity for sustained, supported listening outside the classroom (such as through television or the internet), then about a quarter of the listening and speaking class time could be usefully spent on meaning-focused listening, particularly in the early stages of language learning. Some of this listening may be in the language laboratory if there is one, or from recordings. This will be explored in a later chapter.

Care should be taken to see that the listening covers a range of language uses including fiction and non-fiction, formal and informal, monologue and dialogue, and interactional and transactional. The topics for listening can arise out of the writing programme, the reading programme, or the other subjects studied in the school curriculum such as geography and economic studies.

Here are some examples of how meaning-focused listening was made part of a class's programme.

For young learners, listening was given a high priority.

1. Several days a week learners listened to an interesting story, chapter by chapter (see Chapter 3 of this book for **listening to stories**).
2. The teacher also read to the learners a complete story taken from a "blown up" (very large) book. The learners interacted with the teacher during the reading (see *Teaching ESL/EFL Reading and Writing* (Nation, 2009) for more description of this activity). Often learners heard the same story several times which helped them develop fluency in listening.
3. The learners did guided listening activities like **picture ordering** and **What is it?**
4. The learners did simple group activities where they listened to each other.
5. There was some formal teaching of pronunciation, vocabulary, and grammar.

In an intensive pre-university English proficiency programme, listening was not such a high priority. The learners were living in an English speaking country and had opportunities outside class to watch television, go to films, and communicate with others (native speakers and non-native speakers) in English. The listening parts of the course gave emphasis to listening to formal lectures and talks.

1. Each week a visiting lecturer presented a talk on their speciality. This was prepared for in class by discussion and pre-reading.
2. Recorded radio programmes including news reports were used for repeated listening.
3. Each day there was a receptive information transfer activity covering topics like earthquakes, conservation and health.
4. All classroom management was in English.
5. The learners had access to the language laboratory after class and a wide variety of tapes was available on a library system.

A well-balanced early listening and speaking lesson or series of lessons could contain the following parts.

- *Meaning-focused input.* The learners engage in dialogue with the teacher, do activities like listen and do, grids, interview activities and listening to simple stories.

- *Meaning-focused output.* The learners engage in dialogue with the teacher, do activities like descriptions, a variety of questioning activities like asking by numbers and hints, and guided activities like What is it?, picture stories and the same or different.
- *Language-focused learning.* The teacher helps the learners with pronunciation, memorising useful phrases and sentences, and substitution tables.
- *Fluency development.* Memorised phrases and sentences are given repeated practice with an emphasis on reaching a normal speed of production. The learners listen to the same story several times over several days with the deliveries getting faster. The learners do simple repeated role plays which use the sentences and phrases they memorised and the sentences which they have already practised in substitution tables. They also get very fluent listening to numbers.

CHAPTER **3**
Listening

Why Listening?

> No model of second language acquisition does not avail itself
> of input in trying to explain how learners create second
> language grammars.
>
> (Gass, 1997: 1)

It has been claimed that over 50 percent of the time that students spend functioning in a foreign language will be devoted to listening (Nunan, 1998). Despite this, we often take the importance of listening for granted, and it is arguably the least understood and most overlooked of the four skills (L, S, R and W) in the language classroom.

Listening is the natural precursor to speaking; the early stages of language development in a person's first language (and in naturalistic acquisition of other languages) are dependent on listening. Indeed, Gillian Brown and others (see, for example, Brown, 1978; Brown, Anderson, Shillcock and Yule, 1984) showed that both oracy and literacy development needed ongoing attention in first language education. Prior to this, it was taken for granted that first language speakers needed instruction in how to read and write, but not how to listen and speak because these skills were automatically acquired by native speakers.

Similarly, in second language learning, several writers and researchers in the early 1980s suggested that listening had a very important role (Winitz, 1981). This emphasis on listening was related to a corresponding drop in the importance given to speaking in the early stages of learning, with several writers saying that speaking early in a course should be actively discouraged.

One of the strongest arguments for emphasising listening and delaying speaking is based on a particular view of what it means to learn a language. Some approaches to language teaching have given a lot of importance to speaking. In the very first lesson learners did speaking drills involving repetition and substitution. The lessons involved almost as much speaking as listening, because listening was seen as a way to present models that learners immediately copied. The aim of learning a language was to speak, and language was viewed as a type of behaviour.

Approaches that gave more importance to listening were based on different ideas. Nord (1980: 17) expresses this view clearly:

> Some people now believe that learning a language is not just learning to talk, but rather that learning a language is building a map of meaning in the mind. These people believe that talking may indicate that the language was learned, but they do not believe that practice in talking is the best way to build up this "cognitive" map in the mind. To do this, they feel, the best method is to practice meaningful listening.

In this view of language learning, listening is the way of learning the language. It gives the learner information from which to build up the knowledge necessary for using the language. When this knowledge is built up, the learner can begin to speak. The listening-only period is a time of observation and learning which provides the basis for the other language skills.

What conditions are necessary for language learning to occur? Several writers (Krashen, 1981; Newmark, 1981; Taylor, 1982; Terrell, 1982) using different terminology found considerable agreement. Newmark (1981: 39), for example, said:

> A comprehension approach can work . . . as long as the material presented for comprehension in fact consists of (1) sufficient (2) language instances (3) whose meaning can be inferred by students (4) who are paying attention.

Terrell (1982) and Krashen (1981) would also add that the learner must not feel anxious or threatened by the situation.

Gary and Gary (1981) described the many benefits of delaying speaking and concentrating on listening. These benefits include the following:

1. The learner is not overloaded by having to focus on two or more skills at the same time—a cognitive benefit.

2. Speed of coverage—receptive knowledge grows faster than productive knowledge. It is possible to experience and learn much more of the language by just concentrating on listening. If learners had to be able to say all the material in the lessons, progress would be very slow.
3. It is easy to move very quickly to realistic communicative listening activities. This will have a strong effect on motivation.
4. Learners will not feel shy or worried about their language classes. Having to speak a foreign language, particularly when you know very little, can be a frightening experience. Listening activities reduce the stress involved in language learning—a psychological benefit.
5. Listening activities are well suited to independent learning through listening to recordings.

The comprehension approach had its critics. Some such as Gregg (1984) criticised the logic and research evidence that the approach was based on. Others, such as Swain (1985), suggested that it is not sufficient to result in the kind of learning that is needed to produce the language. All these critics, however, agree that language learning courses should contain substantial quantities of receptive activity. They consider that this receptive activity alone, however, is not sufficient for language learning.

Certainly, most of the early research on comprehension approaches to learning was not well done, and both research and theory now consider that there is an important role for early spoken production in a language course. The effect of the comprehension approach on language teaching has been to highlight the importance of listening and to direct attention to the development of techniques for providing interesting, successful, and sustained opportunities for listening early in a learner's language learning.

Models of Listening

Listening was traditionally seen as a passive process by which the listener receives information sent by a speaker.

More recent models view listening as a much more active and interpretive process in which the message is not fixed but is created in the interactional space between participants. Meanings are shaped by context and constructed by the listener through the act of *interpreting* meaning rather than receiving it intact (Lynch and Mendelsohn, 2002: 194).

Types of Listening

We can distinguish two broad types of listening:

1. One-way listening—typically associated with the transfer of information (transactional listening).
2. Two-way listening—typically associated with maintaining social relations (interactional listening).

Again, we can distinguish traditional, conventional views of listening from more contemporary views. Traditionally, listening was associated with transmission of information, that is with one-way listening. This can be seen in the extensive use of monologues in older listening materials.

While this is fine if we are relating primarily to listening in academic contexts for example, it fails to capture the richness and dynamics of listening as it occurs in our everyday interactions (two-way listening). Most contemporary materials reflect this re-emphasis with a move towards natural sounding dialogues.

Listening Processes

Bottom-up Processes

These are the processes the listener uses to assemble the message piece-by-piece from the speech stream, going from the parts to the whole. Bottom-up processing involves perceiving and parsing the speech stream at increasingly larger levels beginning with auditory-phonetic, phonemic, syllabic, lexical, syntactic, semantic, propositional, pragmatic and interpretive (Field, 2003: 326).

Top-down Processes

Top-down processes involve the listener in going from the whole—their prior knowledge and their content and rhetorical schemata—to the parts. In other words, the listener uses what they know of the context of communication to predict what the message will contain, and uses parts of the message to confirm, correct or add to this. The key process here is inferencing.

When we put these two types of processing together we see listening not as a single skill, but as a variety of sub-skills.

It is possible to make sense of a spoken message by drawing cues from context and picking up a few key words, but without attending to the grammatical form of the message. In other words, comprehension is possible without noticing. This problem with the comprehension approach was identified by Merrill Swain who investigated language development in

French and English immersion programmes in Canada in the 1970s and 1980s (Swain, 1985). She found that English students in French immersion classes were performing as well as French students in subject matter, but their writing and speaking was seriously flawed grammatically despite many hours listening to subjects taught in French.

On the other hand, when we have to say or write something we need to compose the sentence in our head and this involves more attention to grammar; to the syntactic layer of language. So although meaning-focused listening is important, learners also need opportunities to pay attention to language details so they can learn those parts of the language system that may not be so important for basic communication but are important for accuracy.

Meaning-focused listening typically emphasises a top-down approach to listening comprehension. However, Lynch and Mendelsohn (2002), report on a number of recent studies which have shown the importance of bottom-up processing in second language listening.

Tsui and Fullilove (1998) found that more skilled listeners performed better on comprehension questions for which the correct answers did not match obvious content schema for the topic. The implication is that less skilled listeners relied too much on content schemata to assist with guessing. While this helped with items for which the content schemata matched the correct answer, it did not help when there was no match. A second study by Wu (1998) asked learners to think back on how they derived their answers to multi-choice questions in a listening comprehension test. The responses showed that successful comprehension was closely allied with linguistic (bottom-up processing). So evidence suggests that learners need to be proficient with these bottom-up processes and that learners can benefit from being taught how to listen. Lynch and Mendelsohn (2002: 207) suggest the following targets for practice:

- discriminating between similar sounds
- coping with and processing fast speech
- processing stress and intonation differences
- processing the meaning of different discourse markers
- understanding communicative functions and the non-one-to-one equivalence between form and function, e.g., "It's cold in here".

  Form: a declarative sentence structure.
  Function: an imperative function (i.e., requesting that the window be shut or a heater turned on).

Field (2003) also argues for more attention to bottom-up listening skills and presents some detailed proposals for assisting learners with lexical segmentation—with parsing the speech stream so as to distinguish word boundaries. According to Field, three speech phenomena make this particularly difficult for language learners:

1. *Reduced Forms (Contractions, Weak Forms and Chunks)*

   I've lived in Wellington for 10 years.
   Fifty-one high frequency function words in English contain weak forms.
   E.g., been → bɪn, his → z, and → ənd, nd, n (Field, 2003: 334).
   Chunks—*How are you going?*

2. *Assimilation and Elision*

   E.g., [g] or a glottal stop before [k, g], e.g., *good cause → goog cause* (ibid.: 331).
   Typically affects the beginnings and ends of words.

3. *Resyllabification*

   E.g., *went in → wen tin*
   made out → may dout
   (can't) help it → hel pit (ibid.: 332).

Experiences with meaning-focused listening provide a fundamental platform for second language development and content learning. These experiences will usually need to be enriched through directed attention to perceptual processing and parsing skills. Teachers need to find an appropriate balance between providing opportunities for listening skill development through meaning-focused listening and through language-focused learning which focuses on bottom-up listening practice.

Activities for Meaning-focused Listening

In children's classes, the prototypical teacher-fronted listening technique for meaning-focused input is **listening to stories**. The teacher chooses a graded reader that is at the right level for the learners; that is, there are only a few unknown words in the story. The teacher sits next to the whiteboard and slowly reads the story to the learners. Initially, most sentences are read twice and are read slowly. All the time the teacher is watching to see that the learners understand what they hear. When words come up that the learners might not recognise or which might be unknown to the learners, the teacher quickly writes them on the board and gives a quick explanation, using either a translation, a gesture, pointing, a quick drawing, or a simple second language definition. If the same word or another member of its word family occurs again, the teacher points to it on the board. As the learners become familiar with the story the teacher reads a little faster and cuts down the repetitions and explanations. The main goal of the activity is for the learners to follow and enjoy the story. After about ten minutes, the teacher stops at a suitable point, such as the end of a chapter, and the activity ends, to be continued in the next day or so. Listening to the story becomes an eagerly anticipated activity, similar to following a serialised programme on TV.

This technique has the following features.

1. The learners are interested in what they are listening to.
2. They are able to understand what they are listening to.
3. The material is at the right level for the learners.
4. There are a few unfamiliar or partly unfamiliar items that they can understand through the help of context, or through the teacher's explanation. Some of these items occur several times in the input.
5. There is a little bit of deliberate attention given to language features without too much interruption to the flow of the story.
6. There are possibilities for interaction during the listening as the teacher occasionally asks questions or gets the learners to anticipate what will happen, and as the learners ask the teacher to repeat, slow down, or explain.
7. There is a large quantity of input.
8. Learners do not have to produce much output.

Krashen's (1981) claims for the importance of comprehensible input (CI) can be translated into a set of learning conditions; that is, conditions that need to be met for language development through listening. These conditions can be represented by the acronym "M I N U S" and are listed in Figure 3.1.

Conditions	Questions the teacher should ask:
Meaningful	Is the input a piece of meaningful communication?
Interesting	Does the input contain useful or interesting information that will attract the learners' attention?
	What features of the input make it useful or interesting and will engage learners' attention? How are activities associated with listening engaging the learners' interest?
New items	What learnable language, ideas, skills or text types (L I S T) will learners meet through the listening experience?
Understanding	Can the learners understand the input?
	How are the learners assisted with understanding the input (e.g. through controlling the difficulty of the input or through activities that scaffold learning)?
	How are new language items being made comprehensible and how is skill development being scaffolded?
Stress-free	How is stress and anxiety being controlled?

Figure 3.1 Conditions for Learning Through Input

It is useful to keep these conditions in mind when considering the activities that follow.

In **oral cloze** exercises the listeners listen to a story and occasionally (about once every 50 words) the teacher pauses so that the learners can guess the next word in the story. The word should be easy to guess and the guessing should not interrupt the story too much. If the learners can produce very little English, a list of possible words can be put on the board for them to choose from, or they can answer in their first language. Immediately after the learners have guessed, the teacher gives the answer.

In **picture ordering** (Flenley, 1982) the learners see a set of pictures that are in the wrong order. They listen to a description of each of the pictures or to a story involving the events in the pictures, and they put the pictures in the right order. Suitable pictures can be found in picture-composition books or among the comic strips from Sunday newspapers. Instead of using pictures that tell a story, a collection of pictures of faces or cars, for example, can be used. The pictures must be put in the same order as that in which they are described. The same set of pictures can be used again and again with slightly different descriptions and a different order. It is easy to get fluent speakers of English to record descriptions with very little preparation.

The **What is it?** technique (Nation, 1978) has already been described as a way of guiding early listening and speaking. It can also be used to produce large quantities of recorded material for developing the listening skill, and as well is useful as an impromptu technique. The teacher describes something, and the learners have to decide what is being described. The description begins with only a little bit of information, and gradually more and more information is revealed. Here is an example.

> I forgot it when I left home this morning. This made me angry because it is useful. I don't like it very much but I need it. Not every person has one, but I think most people do. Some people like to look at it and now many people play with it. Mine is quite heavy . . .

The rambling description continues with more clues given until the learners guess that a watch is being described. Teachers who are not confident about their own English can follow set patterns when describing.

Same or different exercises can be adapted for listening. Usually in these exercises learners work in pairs, and one member of the pair has a picture that they describe to their partner. The partner tries to decide whether the two pictures are the same or different. They must not show their pictures to each other. When these exercises are used for listening, all the learners have the same picture and the teacher has the other picture. This is just like working in pairs except that the teacher is one member of the pair and the class is the other member of the pair. There are several types of exercises that can be used in this way. The exercises can consist of several small pictures or just a large picture with several differences (see Chapter 6).

Listen and choose exercises are similar to **picture ordering** and **same or different**. The learners listen to a description and choose the picture that is described from a set of similar but slightly different pictures. It is easy to tape-record such descriptions without much preparation so that they can be used for self-study listening. The same sets can be used again and again, by describing different items in the set or getting different people to record descriptions. The descriptions should not be brief; they should add several bits of irrelevant information, should be repetitive, and should be interesting and lively. Brown (1978) suggests that spoken language is used mainly for social reasons and not for conveying detailed information. Where information is conveyed, it is usually given in short bursts. Long, detailed informative pieces of spoken English are uncommon. Accordingly, listening exercises should not be too dense— that is, they should not pack too much information into a single utterance.

There are lots of variations on the **listen and draw** exercise. For the following exercises each learner needs to have a copy of a picture.

1. The learners listen and colour the picture with colours suited to the description.
2. The listeners listen and fill in details on the picture. This can include activities like having an outline of several heads and having to fill in the details of eyes, nose, moustache, scars, mouth and hair while listening to a description of several people. Other activities could involve incomplete maps, rooms, outdoor scenes and cars. A variation of this technique that requires more preparation involves providing small drawings of objects that have to be placed in the right position in a larger picture.
3. The learners listen and label parts of a picture or diagram. The amount of writing required can be reduced by providing a list of the words needed for labelling. I saw this done very well by a teacher telling about her country. The learners had an outline map of the country with some numbered points on it. These points were places. The teacher gave a very interesting description and occasionally indicated when the learners should label the map. This type of activity provides good opportunities for vocabulary learning. For example, the labels can be new words, and the learners discover what objects to label by listening to the description.

Padded questions give a lot of listening practice with a minimal language response. For example, the teacher talks about where she lives and what it is like living there and then asks the learners, "Where do you live?" So each item consists of a simple question which is preceded by quite a long talk on the same topic. Here is another example.

> I don't come from a small family, but I don't come from a big family either. I have one sister. She's the oldest. She plays the piano very well and can drive anything. My two brothers are older than me. All my brothers and sisters are married and have children. How many people are there in your family?

Padded questions are very easy to make because you can talk about your own experience. They can include questions like: Where were you born? What is your job? What's your favourite food? What have you read recently? Do you play tennis?

Supporting Listening

We can assist our learners by providing them with support when they do an activity (e.g., around the house—add a list of words or pictures for the learners to see as they listen). This support acts as a temporary bridge which learners use to reach the target. Over time, learners internalise the expertise required to meet the target independently and the bridge can be removed.

We can provide this support in four main ways:

1. By providing prior experience with aspects of the text (i.e., with language, ideas, skills or text-type).
2. By guiding the learners through the text.
3. By setting up cooperative learning arrangements (for example, shared reading approaches).
4. By providing the means by which learners can achieve comprehension by themselves.

Providing Prior Experience

This can be done by rehearsing the text beforehand, using a simple version first, repeating the listening, using language or ideas already within learners' experience while increasing the skill demands of a task, and pre-teaching items. The topic of the text can come from the learners' previous experience and may be based on a first language text. Similarly, working on a theme that continues over several days can provide useful content support for listening activities, because the learners' content knowledge increases as they keep working on the theme.

Providing Guidance During Listening

Learners can be guided through the text by using completion activities where part of the text is provided but the learners must fill in the gaps, by using ordering activities where the main points are provided and the learners must put them in the correct order, having questions to answer that cover the main points of the input, and having information transfer diagrams to fill in or pictures to label.

Working in Groups to Support Listening

Learners can treat listening as a kind of group work where they are able to negotiate with the person providing the input. This can allow for negotiation to occur during the activity. In note-taking activities learners can work in pairs to take notes, and if the lecturer provides time for learners to discuss the input with each other at points during the lecture this can help those who are getting left behind keep up with what's going on.

Information Transfer

Another group of activities involving a small amount of written language is given the name **information transfer**. In these activities, learners reproduce the message they hear in a new form, for example when they listen and respond by ordering a set of pictures, completing a map, drawing a picture or completing a table. A key characteristic of such activities is that they involve a change in the form of the message but the message remains the same. Listen-and-draw techniques can thus be classified as information transfer techniques. We will now look in detail at information transfer activities.

Most information transfer activities focus the learners' attention on the details of the information used in the activity. There are numerous possibilities. For example, the learners listen to a conversation between a landlady and a new boarder and label a plan of the rooms of the house using the information conveyed in the conversation. Similarly, the teacher talks about her family or an imaginary family and the learners complete a family tree diagram. Palmer (1982) has an excellent list of other suggestions classified according to the type of diagram used. He uses the categories of maps and plans, grids and tables, diagrams and charts, diaries and calendars, and miscellaneous lists, forms and coupons. The following suggestions add to Palmer's examples.

- The learners listen to a report of a robbery and draw the robbers' route through the house on a diagram of the house.
- The learners listen to descriptions of two languages and note their

characteristics on a chart. The chart includes categories like *script, use of stress, word building processes . . .*

- The learners listen to a recorded conversation between a teacher and a parent and put grades and comments on a child's school report.

There are good reasons for using information transfer activities to encourage meaning-focused listening and to support listening. The most obvious learning from information transfer relates to the information in the activity. After doing the activity about the landlady, the boarder and the plan of the house, the learners would be likely to remember the particular plan of that house. So in contrast to the use of comprehension questions, the visual structure of a well-designed diagram for information transfer provides a conceptual scaffold to assist comprehension. Put simply, the visual support makes listening easier.

Second, when used with listening, information transfer focuses learners' attention on listening without the extra burden of having to read a list of questions or write long answers. The principle here is that when the focus is on listening skills, the activity should not require learners to simultaneously read and/or write extensively. Information transfer activities that involve learners tracking a journey on a map, filling in a chart or grid all control the learning burden in this way by requiring minimal response.

Third, these activities can easily be used to draw attention to important and generalisable text structures and information. For example, good note-taking from a lecture presents the ideas in a diagrammatic way that highlights how the ideas relate to one another. (We discuss note-taking in more detail later in this chapter.) Tree diagrams, maps and pictures can reveal the conceptual structure of text types as well as the relationships between parts and between ideas in a text. The more generalisable the text structures that an information transfer activity draws attention to, the more generalisable the learning. This approach trains learners to listen strategically for important information. In other words, the conceptual work that learners must do in a well-designed information transfer activity encourages deep understanding and is particularly good for intellectual development in young learners.

Fourth, information transfer encourages deep processing of input. A key question that teachers should ask about an activity is, "What quality of thinking does this activity promote?" Information transfer requires learners to transform the input in some way, and this typically requires more mental effort than copying or responding to comprehension questions. In a sense then, information transfer activities are *information transforming* activities. It is likely that this deep processing provides good opportunities to learn new vocabulary and grammatical items contained in the spoken or

written text, particularly those items that are focused on in the information transfer activity. Research on vocabulary learning indicates that some
special attention needs to be given to vocabulary if there is to be substantial learning. This can be done either by putting the vocabulary to be
learned in places in the text where most information occurs (Herman,
Anderson, Pearson and Nagy, 1987), or by briefly commenting on particular vocabulary during the storytelling (Elley, 1989). To make the most of
this learning, the vocabulary would need to be high frequency or special-
ised vocabulary which the learners would be sure to need again in their
use of English. Nation (1988) discusses a range of goals for information
transfer activities.

The above four reasons all focus on the role of information transfer in
guiding understanding of input. In addition, information transfer also has
a useful role in pushing learners' production. It does this by providing a
simplified or diagrammatic representation of the original input which
learners can use to "reconstitute" the text in their own words. This can be
represented in the following way:

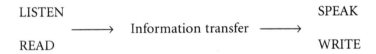

Learners begin by listening or reading, and then completing some kind of
information transfer diagram. They then take part in a speaking or writing
activity in which they retell the main ideas in the text using the diagram as
a guide. In this way, information transfer provides an intermediary bridge
or link between input and output which discourages learners from relying
too heavily on direct copying from the original text, but which still provides them with a conceptual scaffold for rebuilding the original text in
their own words or for another purpose.

Finally, from a practical point of view, information transfer activities
can be much easier to produce than sets of comprehension questions. A
timeline related to a simple narrative, or a simple radio news item
grid such as that below can easily be sketched onto a whiteboard for
learners to copy. Alternatively, the diagram can be described to learners

Table 3.1 Radio News Item Grid

News item	Who	What	Where	When
1				
2				
3				
4				

who then draw it, thus adding another valuable listening opportunity to the activity. The same diagram can become a template to be used regularly in lessons.

Creating Input for Information Transfer Activities

Although listening materials are readily available, these may not always match the particular needs, interests and level of a group of learners. Teachers therefore can greatly enrich listening opportunities through creating topical, custom-made aural texts. Willis (1996) provides a range of excellent ideas for using recordings of spontaneous speech rather than scripted speech in the classroom. Such recordings have the advantage of containing the features of natural speech which learners will encounter outside the classroom. Here is an example of how such a recording can be made and used with an information transfer activity.

You are teaching a group of international students who have arrived in your city to study in an ESOL summer school. They are interested in exploring accommodation options.

1. Cut out a few "to let" ads from the newspaper.
2. Record a conversation between you ("Tom") and a friend ("Ahmed") in which you discuss:
   - information in the various ads and personal preferences regarding this information
   - a ranking of the flats in terms of preference.
3. Design an information transfer table such as Table 3.2 below.

Table 3.2 Information Transfer Table

Location	Place 1 Aro Valley	Place 2 Kelburn	Place 3 Thorndon	Place 4 Mt Cook	Place 5 City central
Number of bedrooms					
Rent cost					
Distance from campus					
Heating					
Date available					
Features					
Ranking Tom					
Ranking Ahmed					

Other topics include movies to see, places to visit, job advertisements, ranking topics such as favourite weekend activities, prediction about the future, favourite books, favourite foods, ways to save money and live cheaply . . . the list is endless!

Most of the activities described above provide some kind of support that makes listening easier. There are several ways of providing this support that can be used across a range of activities.

1. *Listening while reading.* While they listen the learners see the written form of what they are listening to. This can include a written text, a PowerPoint presentation, and captioned movies.

2. *Repeated listening.* There are repeated opportunities to listen to the same text. Repeated reading is a well-established activity for improving reading fluency. Repeated listening using a tape-recorder, DVD or video, or using input from the teacher should also be of value.

3. *Interactive listening.* In a later chapter we will look at interactive activities where learners can control the speed, repetitions and amount of accompanying explanation through interacting with the person providing the input. That is, by asking them to slow down, repeat, clarify, or explain. This broad negotiation can improve comprehension, help learning, and also help develop strategies for dealing with difficult input. Cabrera and Martinez (2001) found that making stories interactional with comprehension checks, repetition and gestures resulted in better comprehension.

4. *Non-linguistic or semi-linguistic support.* Support like information transfer diagrams, pictures and diagrams, OHT or PowerPoint notes, and real objects can all make listening easier if they are directly related to what is being listened to.

Strategies

There is some debate (Ridgway, 2000a and b; Field, 2000) about whether strategy training is useful for listening, although Rubin (1994) claims that listening strategies can be taught and do improve comprehension. To a large degree this debate is about the definition of "strategy", but it does have direct teaching implications. If the here-and-now nature of listening makes strategy use unrealistic then there is little point in training learners in strategies that cannot be applied. Goh (2000) proposes that the first step in strategy training involves finding out the particular problems that learners face in listening comprehension. Here is a list of the problems identified by the learners in her study, who were college level EFL learners in Hong Kong. Learners may have problems with recognising word forms and keeping up with what is coming in. They may also not have enough time to turn perceived form into an appropriate message. While they struggle over one part they may miss what follows. Goh suggests that problems can occur at the levels of perception, parsing and utilisation.

Learners *can* benefit from training in listening strategies. Two types of useful strategies are:

1. *Communication strategies*—strategies to assist comprehension, for example making predictions before listening, listening selectively, knowing how to interrupt politely, etc.
2. *Learning strategies*—strategies for noticing language forms in the input in their independent listening, for example negotiating (seeking clarification), listening for patterns, focused listening.

Advanced Listening: Note-taking

Note-taking is a meaning-focused listening activity. It is also an essential skill for academic study where learners have to attend lectures in another language, but can be used in various forms at all levels of language proficiency.

Note-taking does two jobs: it stores information for later use, and it provides the opportunity to encode information. These two effects are called the storage effect and the encoding effect.

The storage effect of note-taking is the one that most students consider to be important. However, as we shall see later, there are reasons why this effect may not be as important as the encoding effect. Students make use of the storage effect of note-taking when they take notes which they will later use to help recall or revise what occurred in the lecture. Sometimes note-taking of this type is used to make a record of material that is not well understood so that it can later be studied and understood better. This process is helped if a recording of the lecture for repeated listening is also available.

The encoding effect of note-taking occurs at the time the notes are taken. "Encoding" means changing information from one form to another, as in the information transfer activity described earlier. It can mean changing from a written form to a spoken form, for example. It can also mean changing from one form of organisation of the ideas to another form of organisation. For example, it may involve a change from a listing form such as:

1. Skilled reading speed = 25–300 wpm
2. Around 90 fixations per 100 words—200 ms per fixation
3. Saccadic jumps
   (a) 1.2 words per jump on average
   (b) 20 ms per jump

to a diagrammatic form such as:

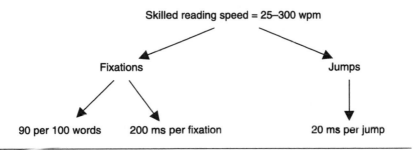

Figure 3.2 Diagramatic Note-taking

Evidence of the importance of the encoding effect is that even with no revision, note-taking helps recall (Barnett, Di Vesta and Rogoszinski, 1981). That is, the activity of encoding or changing the form of the information helps the note-taker to remember the information that they were encoding. This finding fits in with the depth of processing hypothesis which suggests that the most important factor in remembering is not the amount of effort put in to remembering nor the motivation of the learner, but is the depth or thoughtfulness of the mental processing at the time that learning takes place (Craik and Lockhart, 1972). The more thoughtful the mental activity, the better the learning. For example, repeating an item over and over again to yourself is not as deep as trying to find some mnemonic device that you can attach to the item. This means that note-taking works well when learners know thoughtful ways of encoding.

How to Take Notes

Research on note-taking indicates that the best notes are usually taken in the pauses during a lecture. Good note-taking requires time for thought. If the lecturer's style does not provide enough pauses, then after the lecture has ended some time can be used for looking back over notes and reorganising and elaborating them.

The kinds of notes that make best use of the encoding effect of note-taking involve changing the information from a linear form to a form that is organised and patterned in a way that makes sense to the note-taker and that reflects the important relationships between the pieces of information in the lecture. There are several ways of doing this. The most creative is to listen to the lecture and find a unique way of representing the ideas. Buzan's (1974) spray or concept diagrams are a way of doing this (see also Hamp-Lyons, 1983: 120). In this kind of note-taking, the topic is placed in a circle at the middle of the page. Then the various aspects of the topic are attached to the circle and elaborated by lines.

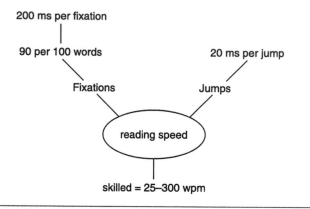

Figure 3.3 Note-taking in a Spray or Concept Diagram

The result is a diagram that changes the linear form of the lecture input to a patterned arrangement that is unique to that lecture. The system is also very flexible as it allows connections to be made between parts which may have been separated in time in the lecture. As Buzan (1974: 87) puts it: "It is the network inside the mind, and not the simple order of word presentation, which is more important to an understanding of the way we relate to words."

Another way of organising note-taking is by relating the information in a lecture to patterns or schema that can be applied to a range of topics. One such set of schemata is Johns and Davies' (1983) topic types. The topic type hypothesis states

> While it is possible to envisage an unlimited range of *topics* which might be identified in ESP texts, there is a strictly limited set of *topic types*. A topic type can be defined by means of its "information constituents"—certain categories of information which consistently co-occur over a wide range of different topics.
>
> For example, the following topics appear on the surface to be quite unrelated: a suspension bridge, a flowering plant, a skeleton, a blast furnace. Nevertheless, in a general sense they are all about the same sort of thing: a *physical structure* of one sort or another. Furthermore, in practice, descriptions of such physical structures consistently provide information which falls into the following categories:
>
> 1. the *parts* of the structure
> 2. the *properties or attributes* of the parts
> 3. the *location* of the parts
> 4. the *function* of the parts.

Moreover, texts describing physical structures not only give information which falls into these four categories or slots, but (virtually) no information of any other kind.

The topic-type **Physical Structure** is one of the set of twelve topic types (Johns and Davies, 1983). See Appendix 2 for the list of topic types.

An advantage of the topic type approach is that the learners become familiar with a generalisable system that reflects the information structure of the topic and discipline that they are studying. This system is of value not only in note-taking from lectures but also in reading and writing.

Another way of organising note-taking is to use very structured approaches like numbered multi-level lists, or tree diagrams. The depth of processing involved in these forms of note-taking depends on the relationship between the organisation of the lecture and the organisation of the notes. The more the notes copy the organisation of the lecture, the less deep the processing.

For some learners taking notes may improve the chances of recall of information, at least because it requires attention, and ideally because it involves thoughtful processing of the information. Not all researchers, however, are convinced of this (Todd, 1996). Generally, short notes are better than long notes because, in shortening, the note-taker has to make decisions about what is important and what can be left out.

Learning How to Take Notes

First, it is worth discussing note-taking with learners, covering the points described above. Information about deep processing is useful not only for note-taking but also for other learning.

Second, it is useful for learners to see examples of various ways of taking notes. A useful procedure after learners have learned about spray diagrams, tree diagrams, and ordered lists is to get one learner to take notes during a lecture on an overhead projector transparency using an OHP pen. At the beginning of the next lecture, the OHP transparency is displayed and both the content and form of the notes are discussed. This has the double effect of providing revision of the previous lecture as well as developing awareness of note-taking skills.

Third, the lecturer can structure lectures to give help with note-taking. This can be done in the following ways.

1. The lecture can be given at a slow rate of delivery with frequent pauses.
2. Several times during the lecture there can be breaks for learners to discuss and compare their notes with their neighbours. These small

discussion groups during a lecture are sometimes called **buzz groups**.

3. The lecturer can use signals to indicate when information is important and should be noted.
4. The lecturer can provide outline sheets or information transfer tables for the learners to complete while listening to the lecture.
5. The learners can read about the content of a lecture before they listen to it. This allows them to focus on the skills of listening and note-taking because they are familiar with the content.

Monitoring Note-taking

Because note-taking is such an individual activity, the most useful monitoring is for learners to look critically at their own note-taking. Here is how this could be done.

1. Learners can compare their note-taking with the note-taking of their classmates. One way of doing this is to use the OHP technique described above. Another way is for the teacher to allow time in lectures for learners to look at their neighbours' notes and to discuss the differences with each other.
2. Learners may be given a checklist to help them evaluate the storage and encoding values of their own notes (see Table 3.3).

Table 3.3 Note-taking Checklist

Why are you taking notes?

- to help remember the lecture content
- to store the lecture content for later study.

To help remember

- Are you putting your own organisation on the notes?
- Are you relating the information to your other knowledge?
- Does the form of your notes help recall the content?

To store the information

- Are your notes clear and well organised?
- Have you chosen the most important information to note down?

Teachers may wish to collect their learners' notes to comment on. This should be for positive comments rather than assessment.

At lower levels of proficiency, note-taking can involve ticking lists of points as they occur, connecting given points by drawing lines between them, having two learners working together to take one set of notes, and completing an incomplete set of notes.

Monitoring Meaning-focused Listening

Examining the Teaching Material

It is useful to examine material before it is used for teaching to see if it is likely to reach the learning goals of the lesson. Figure 3.1 on page 43 provides a set of questions which is useful for checking lesson content. The idea behind this kind of analysis is not that we can plan and account for every piece of learning in a lesson, but that teachers should be purposeful and analytical in their design and use of teaching material. They should be able to say why they are using a particular activity and how its design will help learning.

Observing the Activity

Examining the material before it is used is useful to make sure that the learners' time will be used well. Observing the activity checks if the teacher's predictions were correct by looking for signs that the learning conditions may be occurring.

Table 3.4 A Checklist for Observing a Meaning-focused Listening Activity

1. Were the learners interested in the activity?
2. Did they notice some useful items, and if so, did they

   • quietly repeat them
   • write them
   • respond appropriately to them?

Meaning-focused listening can be a very enjoyable part of the language course. This is especially so if the learners work with interesting material and they have some involvement in the activity. An important skill of the teacher is using interesting material in engaging ways.

CHAPTER 4

Language-focused Learning through Dictation and Related Activities

We can describe dictation as a technique where the learners receive some spoken input, hold this in their memory for a short time, and then write what they heard. This writing is affected by their skill in listening, their command of the language, and their ability to hold what they have heard in their memory. **Dictation** is often associated with more traditional teaching methods, and with testing rather than teaching (Oller and Streiff, 1975; Oller, 1979), however, it remains a valuable teaching technique, and variations on dictation such as **dictogloss** and **running dictation** are very popular with learners and teachers.

Dictations help language learning by making learners focus on the language form of phrase and clause level constructions, and by providing feedback on the accuracy of their perception. There have been no attempts to measure what memory of phrases remains after dictation, so it is safest to regard dictation primarily as a consciousness raising activity. The consciousness raising comes from the subsequent feedback about the errors and gaps in perception.

A dictation text is a piece of connected language about 100 to 150 words long. It is usually chosen so that it is reasonably complete in itself and contains material that suits the level of the learners for whom it is intended. The teacher reads the whole text to the class. Then she reads it again, this time pausing after she reads a group of three to seven words, so that the learners have time to write the words. After the text has been read in this way and the learners have written it, the teacher reads it again without pausing after each phrase but only at the ends of sentences. After this the writing is checked for accuracy. Here is an example of a dictation text. The lines like this / show where the teacher pauses during the second reading so that the learners can write.

> When a person dies/in Bali,/the family and friends/are not usually sad.// For them/death is the beginning/of another life.// The dead person/will come back in the world/in another shape.// Before this happens,/the old body must go.// In some countries,/the dead body/ is put in the ground.// In other countries,/and in some places in Bali,/the body is put/on top of the ground/or in a tree.// The body is then/often eaten by animals.// But usually in Bali,/the dead body is burned.// After it is burned,/the dead person/can easily come back/to live in this world again.// Because of this,/the burning of the body/is a happy time.// When a bad person/comes back to earth,/they may be a dog or a snake.// A good person will have/a better life than the first life.//

The value of a dictation is increased if the learners know what mistakes they made.

Dictation will be most effective when it involves known vocabulary which is presented in unfamiliar collocations and constructions, and when there is opportunity for repetition of the material. The unfamiliar collocations and constructions are the learning goal of dictation. Focusing, holding them in short-term memory, and repetition are the means of learning.

It is easier for the teacher if the learners check their own dictations. The dictation can be written on the blackboard as a model, or printed material can be used. Each learner can check their own dictation, or they can check their neighbour's, or the learners can compare their versions of the dictation in order to agree on a correct version.

Choosing Dictation Texts

A dictation text can be taken from material that the learners have studied before or will study, or it can be taken from other books of a similar level. Usually a dictation text should not contain words that the learners have not met before. Dictation texts should contain useful or interesting content such as that seen in humorous or unusual stories, dialogues and poems. Thornbury (2001: 120–121) provides a useful range of texts for dictation. An amusing dictation involves dictating a puzzle to the learners. After they have written it from dictation they have to solve it. Here is an example.

> There are four people sitting around a table. Three of the people are men—Mr Wood, Mr Williams and Mr Long. One person is a

woman—Mrs X. The woman is the wife of one of the men. Mr Wood sits opposite Mrs X. Mr Long sits to the right of Mrs X. Mr Williams sits at one of the longer sides of the table. Mrs X does not sit next to her husband. Who is the husband of Mrs X? Show the positions of the four people around the table.

Pre-dictation Exercises

Dictation can be used after exercises that provide practice in the words or patterns that are in the dictation and that emphasise the language focus of the dictation activity (Brown and Barnard, 1975). This makes sure that there is a strong focus on wanted constructions, and the eventual dictation becomes more like a learning experience than a test. After one or two of these exercises have been carried out, the learners are given the text as dictation. Here are some typical exercises. After one or more of these exercises have been completed, the dictation is carried out in the usual way.

1. Usually, the dictation text is read once by the teacher before the learners write. This reading helps the learners get a complete view of the dictation.
2. Instead of just hearing the text before it is dictated, the learners can be given the text to read and study before it is dictated. While reading it, the learners can be told to pay particular attention to verb endings, plural *s*, etc. by underlining them. The learners can practise pronouncing the words in the text.
3. Certain types of words from the dictation can be written on the blackboard in the same order as they are in the dictation. The learners are then asked to write the correct form of the words as they appear in the dictation when the teacher reads it, or to write certain words that come in front of or follow those written on the blackboard. For example, the nouns in the text are written on the blackboard. The learners listen to the text and write *a* or *the* or other words that come in front of the nouns. If the nouns are plural in the text, the learners write *s*. Verbs can be written on the blackboard and the learners listen to hear if they have *s*, *ing*, or *ed* on the end and they write the correct form. The teacher should pause often while doing the exercise to give the learners enough time.
4. The teacher tells the learners to listen for all the words ending in *s* (or *ing*, *ed*, etc. or with *the* in front of them, etc.) and to write them.
5. The teacher writes pairs of words on the blackboard. Each pair is two different forms of a word in the text (e.g., *book—books, walk—walked*). The words are written in two columns, a word from each pair in column A and in column B. The words are listed in the same

order as they are in the text. The learners listen to the text and write "A" if they hear the column A word, and "B" if they hear the column B word.

6. The teacher reads the dictation text several times. The learners ask questions about the text and the teacher checks orally if the learners know all the words. After this the text is dictated. The questions that the learners ask should be based on their knowledge of the mistakes they made in other dictations, for example, "Is *country* singular or plural in the first sentence?"

7. The learners are given some questions to answer. They listen to the text and try to find the answers to the questions. The questions can ask about both the grammar and the ideas in the text.

Variations of Dictation

Dictation is an easily prepared activity that can become a part of the regular classroom routine. The following variations can add variety to this routine, and can refocus the learning goal of the dictation activity.

Running Dictation

A short dictation text typed in a large font is posted on the wall outside the classroom. Students work in pairs or small groups. One learner is the writer and the other is the runner who goes to the dictation text, memorises a short sentence, returns to the writer and retells it. If the students are working in groups, the activity takes the form of a relay in which the first runner reads the first sentence of the short text and then runs to another student and tells them what they have read. The second student then runs to a third student and does the same. The third student in turn tells the scribe what they have heard.

If the emphasis is on speaking and listening and not reading and writing, the teacher can sit outside the classroom and say the sentences to the learners. If writing is to be avoided the sentences can be instructions to draw things spoken by the teacher to the runners, for example: For picture one, draw a man carrying five books and a bag of rice; For picture two, draw two girls kicking a ball and a dog chasing a duck.

One Chance Dictation

When learners make very few mistakes in dictation, instead of reading the text several times the teacher can read it only once in short phrases. If the learners know that it will be read only once, it provides a challenge for them to pay attention. If they know that the teacher will read the text several times they might not listen carefully to the first reading.

Dictation of Long Phrases

During the writing part of the dictation, instead of reading short phrases once, the teacher can read long phrases or sentences several times. Each group can be about ten or more words long.

Guided Dictation

Nouns, verbs, adjectives and adverbs are written on the blackboard in the same order as they are in the text. Thus, when the learners listen to the text they can give their attention to the other difficult words. If the words are written in sentence groups as they are in the text, whole sentences instead of phrases can be read at once during the dictation. The words on the blackboard help the learners remember the complete sentences. Here is an example of the words on the blackboard based on the text discussed earlier in the chapter:

> person . . . die . . . Bali . . . family . . . friend . . . usually . . . sad
> *(When a person dies in Bali . . . the family and friends are not usually sad.)*

> death . . . beginning . . . life.
> *(For them death is the beginning/of another life.)*

> Dead . . . person . . . come . . . world . . . another . . . shape
> *(The dead person/will come back in the world/in another shape.)*

If necessary, the teacher can read each group more than once.

Dictation for a Mixed Class

If the class has some learners who are good at dictation and others who are not very good, the teacher can read the text in a special way. She reads the dictation through once without stopping. Then when she reads a phrase for the learners to write, she reads the phrase quite quickly so that the good learners can write it and then she waits a few seconds and reads the phrase again more slowly for the other learners. During the second reading the good learners just check their work. The teacher goes through the dictation, reading each phrase twice in this way.

Peer Dictation

The learners have a copy of the dictation text in front of them. They work in small groups, with one person in the group reading the dictation for the others to write. It may be turned into a competition in the following way. The learners work in pairs. One learner reads a dictation while the other learner writes. They have only a limited time to do the dictation, because as soon as one pair of learners has finished the dictation, they say "Stop!" and the rest of the class must stop work. The learner who is writing can ask the other to repeat words and phrases, and to spell them aloud.

Completion Dictation

The learners are given several printed copies of the text. One copy has a few words missing, the next copy has more words missing, and so on. The learners listen to the text being read by the teacher phrase by phrase and fill in the words missing on their first copy. Then the teacher reads the text again and the learners fill in the missing words on the next copy which has more words missing than the first copy. This continues until the learners are writing the whole dictation. Before the learners fill the words in the second and later copies, they fold their piece of paper so that they cannot see the words that they have already filled in. Here is an example.

1 When _____ person dies _____ Bali, _____ family and friends _____ not usually sad. For them, death _____ _____ beginning of _____ life. _____ dead person will come back _____ _____ world _____ another shape. Before this happens, _____ old body must go.

2 When _____ person dies _____ Bali, _____ family _____ friends _____ _____ usually sad. _____ them, death _____ _____ beginning _____ _____ life. _____ dead person _____ come back _____ _____ world _____ another shape. _____ this happens, _____ old body _____ go.

3 _____ _____ person _____ _____ Bali, _____ family _____ friends _____ _____ _____ sad. _____ _____, death _____ _____ beginning _____ _____ life. _____ dead person _____ _____ _____ _____ _____ world _____ _____ shape. _____ this _____, _____ old body _____ _____.

More and more words are taken out until the learners are writing every word in the text.

Perfect Dictation

After the dictations have been marked, it is usually good for the learners to hear the dictation again while they look at their marked work so they can pay attention to the parts where they made mistakes. Sawyer and Silver (1961) suggest that after the dictation has been marked and returned to the learners, it should be dictated again so that they do not make the same mistakes they did the first time. The dictation is then marked again, either by the learners or by the teacher. It is given again on another day, so that by the time the dictation has been given for the third time, the learners almost know the dictation by heart and are able to write it perfectly. Thus the first marking is only the first step in the teaching and learners will finally produce a perfect copy.

Sentence Dictation

The teacher says sentences and the learners write them. Tucker (1972) suggests that after each sentence has been given as dictation it should be corrected before the next sentence is given as dictation. In this way the learners see their mistakes immediately and can improve during the exercise. The correction can be done by the teacher or a learner writing the sentence on the blackboard and with the learners checking their own work.

Unexploded Dictation

The teacher records a text onto a tape-recorder at normal speaking speed and without the pauses that would normally occur in a dictation. Each working with a tape-recorder, the learners have to make their own transcription of the text, using the rewind and pause buttons on the tape-recorder to keep listening to the text until they can make an accurate transcription. There is now cheap software (http://www.ronimusic.com/leftframe.htm) which allows recordings to be slowed down without changing the pitch. Learners can thus listen to texts that would normally be at too fast a speed for them.

Related Techniques

Dictation is related to several other techniques described below (see Figure 4.1). The main difference between the four techniques is the medium of input and output. Dictation has listening input and written output. Delayed repetition has listening input and spoken output. Read-and-look-up has reading input and spoken output, and delayed copying has reading input and written output. They all involve holding language material briefly in memory before producing it. Let us now look at the techniques other than dictation.

In **delayed repetition**, the learner listens to a long phrase, waits for several seconds, and then repeats it. This technique has sometimes been used as a language proficiency test. This is because the length of the phrase that a learner can hold in memory has been regarded as an indicator of

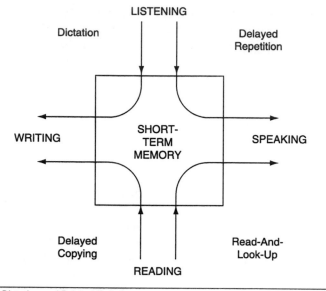

Figure 4.1 Dictation and Related Techniques

language proficiency (Lado, 1965; Harris, 1970). Instead of being an individual test, it can be used as an exercise either with the whole class or in pairs. When it is used as a whole-class activity, the teacher says a phrase, counts to three and then gets the class to repeat it. The length of the phrase is gradually increased and the pause between listening and speaking can also be increased.

The **read-and-look-up** exercise (West, 1960) is a very good preparation for dictation. Remembering a short group of words before reproducing it plays an important part in the read-and-look-up exercise, just as it does in dictation. In the read-and-look-up exercise, the learners work in pairs, one person speaks and the other listens. The one who speaks looks at a phrase in the text, tries to remember it and then looks away from the text and at their partner and says it. They do not speak while reading, and thus must remember what they have read for a short time before saying it. The teacher can break the text into phrases for the learners or they can do it themselves. This technique forces the reader to rely on memory. At first the technique is a little difficult to use because the reader has to discover what length of phrase is most comfortable and has to master the rules of the technique. It can also be practised at home in front of a mirror. West sees value in the technique because the learner

> has to carry the words of a whole phrase, or perhaps a whole sentence, in his mind. The connection is not from book to mouth, but

from book to brain, and then from brain to mouth. That interval of memory constitutes half the learning process . . . Of all methods of learning a language, Read-and-Look-up is, in our opinion, the most valuable.

(West, 1960: 12)

Delayed copying does not involve listening or speaking, but is a part of the set of activities related to dictation. It involves copying from a reading text (Hill, 1969); that is, reading input and writing output. An essential feature of the technique is that the learners try to hold as large a phrase as possible in their memory before writing it. So, instead of copying word for word, the learners read a phrase, look away from the text, and then write it. Unlike dictation, this technique is ideally suited for individual practice.

These techniques can usefully be regarded as variations of dictation, each making use of the same aspect of memory but using different media. There are further variations that can be applied to them. One that can be easily applied to all of them is to provide some written support in the form of the main content words so that a much longer phrase can be held in memory. For example, the words *person, dies, Bali, family, sad*, are always available for the learner to look at while remembering and producing *When a person dies in Bali, the family and friends are not usually sad.*

Monitoring Dictation

When using these techniques teachers should look to see that learners are increasing the size of the span that they are using; that is, the number of words that they can hold in one span. A few experiments with short-term memory in foreign language learning have used memory span as a means of measuring second language proficiency. Lado (1965: 128–129) concluded:

1. Memory span is shorter in a foreign language than in the native language.
2. Memory span in a foreign language increases with mastery of the language.
3. The difference between the native and the foreign language memory span is greater when the material in the foreign language contains the pronunciation and grammatical contrasts between the languages.
4. The relation of memory span to foreign language learning is greater for contextual material than for numbers.

Harris (1970) developed a group-administered memory span test. He found that "the difficulty of the test sentences appeared to be determined very largely by their length and syntactical complexity" (p. 203). Syntactical complexity was determined by the presence of subordinate clauses. Performance on the memory span test "correlated quite highly (from .73 to .79) with performance on standardized listening and grammar tests of English as a foreign language" (p. 203). Research on working memory indicates that people differ in the size of their working memory and that the size of their working memory is a reasonable predictor of vocabulary two years later for young native speakers. There are similar findings for non-native speakers. Typically working memory is measured by seeing how long a string of numbers or letters can be held in memory (Papagno, Valentine and Baddeley, 1991; Atkins and Baddeley, 1998; Service and Kohonen, 1995).

Dictogloss and Related Activities

Dictation and its related activities work mainly at the phrase and clause level. The dictation-based techniques described below work with much larger units of language (see Figure 4.2).

In the **dictogloss** activity (Wajnryb, 1990) learners listen to a short text read twice to them while they take notes. In small groups they reconstruct a written form of the text from these notes. A full description of the steps in the activity is outlined in the table below.

Steps 4 and 5 encourage learners to pay close attention to language form

Table 4.1 Required Steps for a Dictogloss Activity

Step	Students	Teacher
1 Preparation	Vocabulary study activities to prepare for the text. Discuss the topic (predict vocabulary and content etc). Move into groups.	
2 Listening for meaning	Listen to the whole text.	Reads the text at normal speed.
3 Listening and note-taking	Take notes listing key words.	Reads again at normal speed.
4 Text reconstruction in groups	Work in groups to reconstruct an approximation of the text from notes (one learner acts as the writer).	Helps groups. Offers guidance.
5 Text comparison between groups	Compare group versions of the text. Pay attention to points of usage that emerge from the discussion.	Facilitates class comparison of versions from different groups (on OHT or board). Facilitates discussion and correction of errors.

(i.e., word forms, word order, spelling, grammar rules, etc.) within the context of meaning-focused listening and group work. Dunn (1993) cautions that expecting learners to reconstruct a formally identical text may result in strange grammar in the reconstruction as the learners try to fit their notes into the text. This problem may be solved through having long texts, encouraging the learners to take non-linear notes, and expecting an interpretive summary rather than an exact reconstruction.

Mayo (2002) also found that learners appeared more concerned with producing a coherent paragraph than discussing specific issues of language expression. To encourage greater attention to form, she suggests that teachers need to pay close attention not only to the choice of task, but also to the way learners interpret and perform the task. Wilson (2003) suggests adding a "discovery" step to the dictogloss activity to improve learners' perception of spoken language. In this step, learners compare the reconstructed text and the original and notice the types of errors that got in the way of understanding the text. Learners classify their errors using the following list:

What problems did you have:
    a I couldn't hear which sound it was.
    b I couldn't separate the sounds into words.
    c I heard the words but couldn't remember their meaning quickly enough.
    d This word was new to me.
    e I heard and understood the words but not the meaning of that part of the sentence.
    f Other problems . . . (Wilson, 2003: 340).

According to Wilson, by comparing these examples with the original text, learners became aware of four learning points:

1. Recognising common word combinations.
2. Discovering how known words actually sound in context and in unfamiliar collocations.
3. Becoming more familiar with certain grammatical points and words.
4. Discovering how top-down inferencing might have helped resolve specific problems.

Dicto-comp

The dicto-comp (Ilson, 1962; Riley, 1972) is similar to the dictogloss, but does not involve group work. In the dicto-comp, the learners listen as the teacher reads a text to them. The teacher may read it several times. Then, the learners write what they can remember without any further help. The main difference between dictation and the dicto-comp is that in dictation the learners have to remember a phrase of several words as accurately as possible. In the dicto-comp the learners have to remember the ideas in a text of more than one hundred words long and express them in the words of the original or in their own words. The dicto-comp, whose name comes from *dictation* and *composition*, reduces the cognitive load of a task (in this case a writing task) by preparing the learners well before they do the task. In dicto-comp and its related techniques, the preparation provides the learners with ideas, language items, and text organisation so that they can focus on the skill aspect, which, for dicto-comp, is writing.

Related Techniques

Figure 4.2 shows how the dictogloss and dicto-comp are related to other techniques.

The input to **retelling** is reading. Different learners can read different texts, or a single text can be divided in half or into sections with groups of learners responsible for reading and retelling their section to the others. For example, in a class of 20 learners, a text can be divided into four sections with each section read by one of four groups of five learners. These "**expert groups**" read their section of text cooperatively and rehearse their understanding of the text. They then put away the text and recombine into five new groups of four made up of one member from each

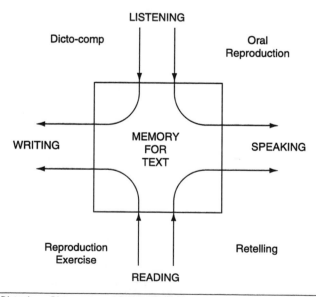

Figure 4.2 Dictogloss, Dicto-comp and Related Techniques

of the previous groups. In these new groups each member retells or summarises their section of text from memory, and so the full text is reconstructed orally.

If each learner has a different text, the retelling can combined with the 4/3/2 technique (Maurice, 1983), where the same information is told by the same person three times. Each time, however, it is told to someone who has not heard it before and with less time (four minutes, then three minutes, then two minutes) to retell it. This results in increasing fluency in the retellings (Nation, 1989a; Arevart and Nation, 1991).

Elkins, Kalivoda and Morain (1972) in an interesting article called "The fusion of the four skills" describe a chain procedure where information is read then spoken then written. This procedure is simply the activities of retelling and dicto-comp chained together and repeated. Elkins et al. intend that there should be a different person at each part of the chain, but there are advantages for the development of fluency if the chain is a circle of three people who have to process the same information several times in a different medium.

The **reproduction exercise** involves reading input and written output. The learners read a text and then have to produce their own written version of it without looking back at the original. The learning benefits of this exercise can be increased if the learners are required to fill in an information transfer diagram after reading the text. The diagram can be based on the information in the text using a topic type analysis (Franken, 1987). Thus a diagram for a text of the characteristics topic type (Johns and Davies, 1983), such as a description of contact lenses or the baobab tree, would look like Table 4.2.

Topic types are dealt with in detail in the companion volume to this book, *Teaching ESL/EFL Reading and Writing*.

In the **oral reproduction** activity, the teacher tells the class that he is going to say a dialogue (with a learner) and that he is going to say it only once. After he has said it, the learners must repeat the dialogue correctly. Then the teacher says the dialogue. The learners cannot see the dialogue written anywhere. Then the teacher asks the class to tell him

Table 4.2 Information Transfer Diagram for the Characteristics Topic Type

Group Example(s) Features	Tests or evidence of features
1	1
2	2
3	3
4	4

the first line or first word in the dialogue. When someone in the class has told him correctly, the teacher repeats these words and then asks for the next word or line. This continues until the whole dialogue is built up again. This works very well for a big class. As the aim of this technique is to get the learners to memorise the dialogue, the teacher should try to repeat the material the learners have said as many times as he can. If the class has difficulty remembering the next word, the teacher can say the word without making any sound so that the learners must read his lips, or he can pretend that a learner at the back of the class has said the word. This exercise works especially well with a large class. Poems and songs can be used as interesting material for memorisation. They should contain common words and sentence patterns, and should follow the stress patterns of ordinary spoken English (Coe, 1972). The following Robert Frost poem is an example of a poem with these regular features. There are many songs that can be used but not so many poems (Richards, 1969).

Fire and Ice

Some say the world will end in fire,
Some say in ice.
From what I've tasted of desire
I hold with those who favor fire.
But if it had to perish twice,
I think I know enough of hate
To say that for destruction ice
Is also great
And would suffice.

For an easier variation, the teacher reads the complete dictation text once. Then she reads it again but this time she leaves out some words. The learners try to replace those words orally.

Disappearing text is a version of **oral reproduction**. The teacher writes a relevant text on the blackboard. Usually the text should contain about 50 or 60 words, but this depends on the ability of the class. She asks a learner or two to read it. Then she rubs out some of the words. It is usually best to rub out words like *a, the, in, of, I, he*, etc. at the beginning. Then she asks another learner to read it aloud. The learner must supply the missing words as they read. Then some more words are rubbed out, another learner reads, and this continues until there is nothing at all on the black-board, and the learners are saying the dialogue from their memory. It is best not to rub out too many words each time so that many learners have a chance to read the text. If someone makes a mistake while reading, the class corrects them (Nation, 1975). The aim of the technique is to get the learners to repeat the material correctly as many times as possible so that it will be memorised. To get more repetitions the teacher can divide the class in half. As words are rubbed out one learner from each group reads. So this gets two readings for each rubbing out. In a beginners class this works well with simple dialogues or with substitution tables.

In the **phrase by phrase** activity, the teacher reads the dictation to the learners phrase by phrase. After reading a phrase the teacher points to a learner and that learner has to repeat that phrase from memory. If a learner makes a mistake the teacher repeats the phrase again. If the learners can do this easily the teacher says a phrase and then waits for five seconds before asking a learner to repeat the phrase. Thus, the learners have to keep the phrase in their memory for a longer time.

Dictation-based techniques such as dictogloss can be designed to suit learners at a wide range of proficiency levels. Aside from the content and language difficulty of the text, the main factors influencing the degree of challenge in the activity, are:

- the number of repetitions, speed or time that the learners have to comprehend and retain the input
- the length of the delay between the input and the production of the output
- the degree of detail and resemblance of the input expected in the output.

These factors can all be played one against the other. So, in a dictogloss, the text may be spoken quite quickly but with several repetitions. Alternatively, the text may be spoken quite slowly and with several repetitions, but the learners are expected to write something that quite closely resembles the original.

The techniques described here have both language learning and skill learning goals. The language learning goal is met when the activity provides opportunities for learners to notice particular language features and to meet these features a number of times. This goal is also met in the dictogloss activity when learners engage in language of the discussion of the text they are reconstructing. The skill learning goal is met as learners improve bottom-up listening skills, such as familiarity with the sound of word combinations, and top-down skills, such as making inferences based on deduction, previous information or background knowledge.

CHAPTER 5

Pronunciation

When some teachers and learners complain about difficulties in speaking, they are often talking about pronunciation. The amount of attention given to the teaching of pronunciation in language courses varies considerably, partly as a result of the teacher's attitude to error and the learners' language learning goals.

The Importance of Pronunciation

Having a good pronunciation of the language can help in normal communication, particularly intelligibility (Derwing and Munro, 2005). However, that is not the only reason for developing a stable pronunciation of a new language. There is a very important mechanism involved in working memory called the phonological loop. In essence, the phonological loop is the brain saying a word or phrase over and over to itself in order to keep it in working memory or to help it move into long-term memory. A good example of this is the way we say a telephone number over and over to ourselves in order to keep it in memory while we go about dialling the number. If learners do not have a stable pronunciation for a word, it cannot easily enter long-term memory because it cannot be held in the phonological loop (Ellis and Beaton, 1993; Baddeley, Gathercole and Papagno, 1998; Singleton, 1999: 148–151). Learners differ in the amount of information that they can hold in the phonological loop at one time. This amount of information correlates reasonably well, both for native speakers and non-native speakers, with vocabulary size a few years later (Papagno,

Valentine and Baddeley, 1991; Service, 1992; Service and Kohonen, 1995). For second language learners it is likely that the size of their working memory in the second language is affected by their knowledge of patterns of pronunciation and grammar in that language. It is thus important that attention is given to pronunciation in the course so that learners can quickly develop a stable pronunciation, and become familiar with the patterns and rules that work within the second language. Although native speakers cannot explain these patterns and rules, they are able to indicate which are permitted within their language and which are not. Second language learners need to develop these same intuitions.

The Place of Pronunciation Instruction

The theme of this chapter is that it is important to have a broad view of what is involved in pronunciation and what is involved in learning a new sound system. This chapter deals with language-focused ways of trying to develop pronunciation. Trofimovich and Gatbonton (2006) show there is value in giving deliberate and repeated attention to spoken features. As will become clear from the first part of this chapter, pronunciation is affected by a wide variety of factors. Being able to consciously perceive and produce the spoken form is only one of these. Some teachers reject any type of form-focused pronunciation teaching, but this is probably short-sighted. Appropriate attention to form for pronunciation is likely to have the same kinds of good effects as attention to form can have for the learning of vocabulary, grammar or discourse. As with all instruction, it is necessary to find a suitable balance between the four strands of opportunities for learning described in Chapter 1 of this book.

In their review of the status of pronunciation in language teaching, Pennington and Richards (1986) look at a range of factors that should be considered as a part of pronunciation. Pronunciation includes the articulation of individual sounds and the distinctive features of sounds like voicing and aspiration, voice-setting features (Esling and Wong, 1983), and stress and intonation. Attention to these aspects also requires attention to the blending and omission of sounds, and the effect of the various aspects on intelligibility. Thus, although it can be very useful to provide practice with individual sounds, it is also important to give attention to other aspects of the sound system.

In trying to change the fossilised pronunciation of advanced ESL learners, Acton (1984) also took account of a wide range of factors. First, he placed much of the responsibility for change on the learners, requiring them to make the best use of their time out of class and to find opportunities for making pronunciation changes in their spontaneous speech.

Second, he gave a lot of attention to helping the learners to deal with their attitudes and feelings as these affect their pronunciation. Third, he helped learners with the non-verbal behaviours associated with pronunciation like facial expression and gesture. Fourth, Acton provided opportunity for the controlled practice of sounds in formal exercises. Fifth, the learners were encouraged to make use of written pronunciation guides in dictionaries so that their pronunciation could be helped by conscious knowledge of the written form. There were other features in Acton's programme but what is most notable is the wide range of factors that he considered when designing his programme.

In this chapter we will look at the goals of pronunciation practice, the factors affecting pronunciation, the procedures and techniques that teachers and learners can use to improve pronunciation, and the place of pronunciation in a course.

Goals

There continues to be debate about whether the model for foreign language learners should be native-speaker or non-native-speaker English, and if native-speaker English, should it be British, American or some other regional pronunciation. Once political issues have been considered, the usual approach is to set up a list of criteria that typify a good pronunciation (Brown, 1989). These criteria include intelligibility (Abbott, 1986) (to both native speakers and non-native speakers), identity (does the pronunciation identify the speaker with others he or she would like to be identified with?), ease of learning, acceptability by parents and the educational administration, and the availability of teachers and materials to support the wanted pronunciation. In reality, this most often means that local pronunciations of English become the norm for the majority of learners. As we shall see later, Stevick (1978) considers pronunciation and personal identity to be very closely related, and any teacher that ignores this could spend a lot of wasted effort on an unattainable goal. Levis (2005) describes the nativeness principle which sets a native-speaker goal for learners, and the intelligibility principle which accepts accents and sets understanding as the goal. Jenkins (2002) argues that intelligibility must be the main criterion and describes what she calls "the Lingua Franca Core" which consists of the phonological and phonetic features that "seem to be crucial as safeguards of mutual intelligibility" in interlanguage talk. These include most of the consonant sounds with some provisos, initial consonant clusters, the distinction between long and short vowels, and the placement of contrastive stress. Jenkins' proposal is a very pragmatic approach to setting pronunciation goals, and provides very useful guidelines for teachers of elementary and intermediate students.

Factors Affecting the Learning of Another Sound System

There are five factors that have been shown to have major effects on the learning of another sound system. They are the age of the learner, the learner's first language, the learner's current stage of proficiency development, the experience and attitudes of the learner, and the conditions for teaching and learning. All these factors need to be considered in a well-balanced approach to pronunciation.

Age

There is clear evidence that there is a relationship between the age at which a language is learned and the degree of foreign accent (Patkowski, 1990). Usually, if the learner began to speak in the second language before the age of six there will be little or no accent. If the learner began to speak between the ages of seven and 11, the learner is likely to have a slight accent. If the learner began to speak after the age of 12, then there is almost always an accent (Tahta, Wood and Lowenthal, 1981a and 1981b). There are two important points to note here. First, this relationship between age and accent does not invariably apply to everyone. A few adult learners do achieve native-like pronunciation. Second, there are several competing explanations of the cause of the relationship. The physical explanation says that there are physical changes in the brain as a result of age that affect the learning of a new sound system and other aspects of the language. Researchers are reluctant to accept this explanation (Flege, 1987; Patkowski, 1990). The intellectual explanation says that learners have already learned the sound system of their first language and this increasingly disrupts their perception of a second and later language. Age affects this perception because the first language system becomes increasingly well-integrated and stable as learners get older (Flege, 1981). The psychological explanation says that pronunciation is a part of our personality and as we become older we become more protective of our personality and unwilling to change it (Stevick, 1978; Guiora et al., 1972a and 1972b). Perhaps the clearest example of this is the unwillingness of many teenagers to publicly pronounce the unusual sounds of a new language particularly in the presence of their friends. One of the most ingenious tests of this explanation was carried out by Guiora and his colleagues (1972a) who got learners to drink some alcohol to see if its relaxing effect would positively affect learners' pronunciation. They found that drinking a certain amount of alcohol did result in an improved pronunciation. The classroom implications of this are unsettling!

The intellectual and psychological explanations are not in conflict with each other. For a teacher it means that these factors have to be considered when designing a lesson and a programme.

Stevick (1978) combines these two explanations. Stevick believes that learners are easily able to copy new sounds, but there are three reasons why they might have difficulty.

1. *They overlook some feature.* If this happens the teacher can help by giving a suitable model which is not too difficult for the level the learners have reached and by making it easy for the learners to find out how near their pronunciation is to the standard set for the course. This addresses the intellectual aspect.

2. *The learners sound bad to themselves when they copy well.* People are usually sensitive about their pronunciation because it allows others to guess their social background. Also, if learners' pronunciation of a foreign language is very good, others may think it is because they love the foreign culture and want to be like the foreigners. It might also be that the sounds or other features of the foreign language (e.g., tones, stress, sounds like [ð], [f]) sound very strange to the learners and so they may not want to copy them correctly even though they can. Learners' pronunciation will improve when they feel more comfortable about the way they sound when they speak the foreign language and when they develop positive attitudes towards the native speakers of the foreign language.

3. *The learners become anxious about making the sounds.* If the teacher points out to the students that they are not saying something correctly, they may become very tense and nervous and be unable to do it correctly. The teacher thus needs to find ways of helping learners find out what their pronunciation is like without getting them worried about it.

Stevick's approach sees the learning of pronunciation as only one aspect of a total process, mainly social in nature, which involves the whole learner and not just the speech apparatus or intellectual understanding.

The Learner's First Language

Teachers' experience and research studies show that the learners' first language can have a major influence on learning the sound system of another language. The type of evidence for this is where speakers of the same first language typically pronounce the second language in the same way, making the same kinds of substitutions and patterns of pronunciation.

Another type of evidence is that there is a reasonable degree of predictability in the types of relationships between first language and second language sounds and their relative difficulty for long-term success for second language learners. Hammerly (1982), for example, gives the following list of relationships ranked from the most difficult to the least difficult.

- The first language has an allophone not in the second language (Samoan [t]).
- The second language has an allophone that is not in the first language (dark [l], aspiration).
- The second language has a phoneme that is not in the first language (/ð/).
- The learner has to use a first language phoneme in a new position (final /t/ for Chinese speakers).

Flege and Port (1981) also found "the most important interference from 1L to 2L occurs at the level of phonetic implementation rather than at an abstract level of organisation based on features" (p. 125). This indicates that rather than giving attention to general features such as voicing or aspiration, a teacher should be giving attention to the particular sounds where these problems occur.

Teachers can take account of first language influence by being familiar with the sound system of the learners' first language and thus gaining some idea of the amount of effort and attention needed to bring about a wanted change. Later in this chapter a procedure for looking at the difference between wanted and unwanted sounds is described so that this knowledge can be used to help in pronunciation practice. Familiarity with first language sounds can help considerably in this procedure as unwanted sounds often show a first language influence.

The Learner's Development and Range of Styles

There is considerable evidence to show that a learner's pronunciation changes as the learner becomes more familiar with the second language (Major, 1987). Just as there is an interlanguage stage for grammatical development there is a developmental interlanguage stage for phonology. Major (1987: 196) suggests that as learners proceed in their learning of the second language, interference processes from the first language decrease but developmental processes increase and then decrease. This means that teachers should not classify learners' pronunciations too quickly as errors, but should look to see if they are stable or changing. If they are stable, there may be value in encouraging change. If they are changing it may be better just to observe. Change may also be seen by observing learners' pronunciation in formal and informal situations, as different styles of pronunciation may be used. The presence of different styles shows flexibility and shows that the learners' second language pronunciation is developing. Before beginning intensive pronunciation work, it is thus useful to observe learners over a period of time and in a range of situations.

The Experience and Attitudes of the Learner

Each learner brings different life experience and attitudes to the classroom and these may affect the learning of a new sound system. Purcell and Suter (1980) looked at 20 different factors that might affect learning. These included experience factors like the number of years the learner had lived in an English-speaking country, the amount of conversation at home in English, the amount of training to speak English, the number of languages the learner knew, and the proportion of teachers who were native speakers. They also included attitude factors like the type of motivation (economic, social prestige, integrative) of the learner, the strength of the learner's desire to have an accurate pronunciation, the learner's skill at mimicry, and the learner's extroversion or introversion. Purcell and Suter found that the factors most strongly related to success in pronunciation were the number of years the learner had lived in an English-speaking country, the number of months the learner had lived with native speakers, the learner's first language, the learner's desire to have an accurate pronunciation, and the learner's skill at mimicry. In general, it was found that classroom factors, like the quantity of English lessons and whether the teachers were native speakers, were not important factors.

The Conditions for Teaching and Learning

The ways in which the sound system is taught and learned can have effects on learning. The following findings can be useful guides to classroom practice.

- Sounds which are tested in known words and phrases are mispronounced more frequently than the same sounds in unknown words and phrases (Hammerly, 1982). This means that when correcting learners' pronunciation it is better to practise the sounds in nonsense words or in unfamiliar words. If this is not done, there is likely to be interference from previous errors. Similarly, Hammerly (1982) found that problem sounds were more often mispronounced in cognate words than in non-cognate words. This means that for an Indonesian, for example, using the English word *lamp* to practise /æ/ would cause problems because of the cognate word *lampu* in Indonesian where the first vowel is /aː/. It is easier to pronounce a problem sound if it is in a word that does not bring other sound associations.
- The written form of a word can affect its pronunciation. Hammerly

(1982) found that reading aloud was more difficult than imitating for correct pronunciation if the spelling system was misleading. Dickerson (1990) presents evidence that shows that sometimes the spelling system may provide a more effective basis for rules of pronunciation, for example for -s and -ed suffixes, than the phonological system itself. Teachers need to look carefully at the positive and negative effects of spelling on pronunciation when carrying out a pronunciation activity.

- Tongue-twisters like "Round the rugged rocks the ragged rascal ran" or "She sells sea shells on the sea shore" are very difficult for native speakers of English. For learners of English as a second language they are a cruel and unusual punishment.
- Seeing a speaker's mouth movements can have a significant effect on listening (Kellerman, 1990). While tapes may be useful for developing certain aspects of pronunciation, there should also be opportunities to see and listen.
- Jenkins (2002) argues that communication activities between learners with different first languages are a good way of encouraging intelligibility. Such tasks make learners focus on intelligibility in order to get their message across, are meaningful, and avoid the embarrassment of teacher correction.

Procedures and Techniques

As we have seen, there are many factors to be considered when learning a new sound system. As a result, there are many techniques and procedures that can be used to focus on various aspects of the pronunciation task and to take account of the various factors affecting pronunciation. Here we will look at techniques and procedures that focus on the articulation of particular sounds, and stress and intonation.

Articulation of Individual Sounds

Strevens (1974) suggests that most learners are able to mimic particular sounds without any special teaching. The following procedure moves from mimicry through observation and explanation to rather drastic forcing techniques. Practice with individual problem sounds is important and informed teachers can bring about significant improvement in their learners' pronunciation with such practice (Pennington and Richards, 1986: 217). Usually such practice is based on observation, analysis and selection by the teacher, and may begin with getting learners to hear the differences between sounds and to identify particular sounds before they are guided in pronouncing them.

Learning New Sounds: A Procedure

Before teaching or correcting a sound, certain information is needed. Then the teacher can follow several steps to teach the sound.

Necessary Information

(a) Does the learner have the wanted sound in the first language? What is the nearest sound?
(b) What sound does the learner put in place of the wanted sound?
(c) Does the learner make this mistake in initial, middle, and final position?
(d) What is the difference between the wanted sound and the unwanted sound? This can be analysed using a table like this. The table has been filled in for the wanted sound /w/ and the error /v/.

Sounds	Voicing	Place (1)	Place (2)	Type
/w/	voiced	top lip	bottom lip	semi-vowel
/v/	voiced	top teeth	bottom lip	continuant

Teaching the Sound

(a) Teach the learner to *hear* the wanted sound by using distinguishing and identifying activities. (Compare it with the sound the learner usually puts in its place, and other sounds that are like it both in the first language and the foreign language.) Distinguishing should come before identifying.
(b) Give advice and help to get the learner to make the sound. Practise the sound by itself or in easy syllables. The first step is for the learners to repeat the sound copying the teacher. If this is not successful, learners can be helped to pronounce sounds if the teacher explains the position of the tongue and lips, and explains what type of sound it is. If the learners still cannot make the sound after trying to copy the teacher and listening to the explanation, there are several techniques that they can use to force their mouths to the correct position. The technique that is used often depends on the type of mistake that the learners make. For example, if a learner says /f/ instead of /v/, the teacher has to make the learner voice the sound. If a learner says /w/ instead of /v/, the type of correction is different; the teacher has to get the learner to push their lips to the correct position. So the teacher should look carefully at the type of error before deciding what technique to use for forcing. Here are some examples of simple descriptions and forcing procedures.

/f v/   /f/ is a voiceless continuant. /v/ is a voiced continuant. The bottom lip touches the top teeth.

Push a pencil against the bottom lip to bring it forward to touch the top lip. Bring the top teeth down to touch the bottom lip. Make a long sound. If the two lips touch each other, lift the top lip with your own hand. This stops the two lips from touching.

/r/   /r/ is a voiced continuant sound. The end of the tongue is near the top of the mouth. The tongue should not touch the tooth ridge.

Put a finger or a pencil *under* the tongue. Push the tongue back and up. The pencil should go about 5cm into the mouth. Be sure the tongue does not touch the top of the mouth. The pencil stops the tongue from touching the tooth ridge. Make a long sound.

When the teacher pronounces a sound, the learners should watch the teacher's mouth carefully. Then they can practise using a small mirror so that they can see their own mouth.

It is valuable to let the learners experiment with sounds. By changing the position of their tongue they can change the sound. (This is useful for /s/ and /š/.) By changing the position of the lips and teeth the sound can be changed. Activities like these may help the learners to be able to feel where their tongue is in their mouth. This is a useful ability when learning a new language.

(c) Practise the sound in other positions. Consonant groups should come last of all.

Teaching the sound usually begins with hearing practice because it is believed that such practice also improves pronunciation (Henning, 1966). A good technique for practising hearing is easy for the learners to understand, tells the teacher quickly and easily if the learners can recognise the sounds, and gives most of the class some practice.

Hearing Sounds

To help learners in **distinguishing sounds**, the teacher says a pair of words (they can be nonsense words). Sometimes the two words are the same, *pa—pa*. Sometimes they have one sound different, *pa—ba*. The learners listen and if they think that the two sounds are the same, they say "the same". If they are different, they say "different". Learners answer individually when the teacher points to them, or the learners can move their right hands when the two sounds are the same and do nothing when they are different. Briere (1967) found that learners preferred to answer "the same" rather than "different" when they were not sure of the correct answer. Thus, in such exercises many of the correct answers should be "different".

In the **identifying sounds** activity, the teacher writes two words on the blackboard and draws a hand next to one of the words.

fa   (picture of a hand)
pa

Whenever the teacher says a word which begins with the same sound as the word with the picture of the hand next to it, all the learners must move their right hand. If the teacher says a word which begins with the other sound (the one which does not have the picture of a hand next to it) the learners do nothing. This gives all the class practice and the teacher can easily see who can hear the sound. Later during the exercise the learners can shut their eyes so they do not copy the others but give all their attention to hearing. One of the most important parts of hearing practice is telling the learners whether they are correct or not. The teacher should give plenty of examples first and move her hand herself in the beginning, to help the learners. The learners should practise hearing the sound in all positions in the syllable. There are various ways of responding in this activity. Instead of moving their hands, the learners can say, write, or point to a number;

1 fa
2 pa

or a letter f or p.

In **identifying sounds using pictures**, the learners see two pictures, for example, one showing a sheep and another showing a ship. When the teacher says "a sheep" the learners must point to the correct picture. This exercise is used with pairs of words that are the same except for one different sound, for example, *watching—washing, chair—share, live—leave*, etc. In order to give all the class some practice, the teacher should put the two pictures far apart at opposite ends of the blackboard. Then, the teacher can easily see who is pointing to the wrong picture.

The pairs of words can be put in sentences: "I see a ship. I see a sheep." It is often difficult to make matching pairs of sentences like this, but it makes an amusing classroom exercise. Learners can give answers to the sentences to show that they hear them correctly.

"I see a ship."   Answer "It's in the port."
"I see a sheep."   Answer "It's eating grass."

When the learners are trying to hear the difference between sounds, it is best for the sounds to be alone or in nonsense words (Jones, 1960). In each pair of sounds, one sound can be from the first language and the other from English, or they can both be English sounds. Words that are already known to the learners or that have a meaning for them should be avoided. The meaning of the words may take the learners' attention away from the sounds, and their past failure to make the sounds correctly in those words could increase difficulty (Wintz and Bellerose, 1965). During some hearing exercises, learners can close their eyes while they listen, or the teacher can hide her mouth with a piece of paper.

In **don't be tricked**, some words are written on the blackboard. A learner points to one of them. The teacher pronounces it. Sometimes the teacher pronounces the wrong word. The learners must say if the teacher is right or wrong. So, *pa* and *fa* are written on the blackboard. The learner points to *pa*. If the teacher says *fa*, the learners say "no". The learners listen carefully because they know that the teacher will sometimes try to trick them.

In **keep up**, some words that are only a little different from each other are written on the blackboard.

fa
pa
ba

While the teacher says the words quite quickly a learner tries to point to them. Or, each word has a number in front of it. The teacher says the words in a different order and the learners write the numbers in the same order as the teacher says them.

Multiple-choice sounds involves the learners seeing a list of groups of five words.

1 heat   hit   eat   hat   it
2 can   kin   ken   gone   Kim

The teacher says one word from each group and the learners draw a circle around the word that the teacher said. The same list can be used several times. When the teacher has gone through the list once, she can say to the learners, "Now we will start at number 1 again. This time draw a square around the words that I say." Then, the teacher says words that she did not say the first time.

In **triplets**, the teacher says three sounds or words one after the other, for example, "fa pa pa". The learners must answer 2, 3, because two and three are the same. If the teacher says "fa pa fa", the learners must answer 1, 3, because one and three are the same. The learners can write their answers or say them. If all the sounds are the same, the learners answer 1, 2, 3. Briere (1967) found that if the two sounds that are the same are next to each other, fa fa pa (1, 2), or fa pa pa (2, 3), it is easier for the listeners than if they are not next to each other, fa pa fa (1, 3). Denham (1974) also found that the arrangement had an effect on the difficulty, although her results were slightly different from Briere's. It seems that in this exercise, memory is also important.

The same technique can be used for four sounds or words, but then memory becomes even more important.

For **sound dictation**, the teacher says nonsense words or new words and the learners write them. If the learners write them correctly, it shows that the learners can hear the words correctly. Another way is that the vowels are given numbers. When the learners hear a word containing a vowel they write the number of the vowel. The different vowels can be given with the same consonants to make hearing easier (Allen, 1972).

Pronouncing to hear works on the idea that learning to produce new sounds may improve the learners' ability to hear them correctly. The learners may experiment in pronouncing the sounds with the teacher guiding them. They can be shown the position of the tongue and copy the teacher's pronunciation. There is no rule that hearing practice must come before speaking. Teachers should experiment to see what way is best for certain learners and certain sounds. Learners can be taught to pronounce some sounds correctly before they can hear the difference between these sounds and others (Briere, 1968).

Similarly, a description of certain sounds can help the learners to hear the sounds correctly. Learners need help *before* they listen, not just correction after they have heard incorrectly (George, 1972). For example, the teacher can describe the difference between two sounds and draw the learners' attention to the important parts of the sounds. So, before giving hearing practice in distinguishing /ð/ and /d/ the teacher can point out that /ð/ is a longer sound than /d/, /ð/ is a continuous sound while /d/ is like a small explosion. This description is often best given in the first language.

Producing Sounds

In the **repeating sounds** activity, the teacher says the new or difficult sounds. The learners listen and repeat. Locke (1970) found that after a learner had copied a model to pronounce a new sound twice, there was very little further improvement. That is, after repeating the sound for the second time the learners did not usually make any more improvement even though they heard the same model and tried to copy it several times. This means that repeating after the model is only useful for a short time. If the teacher wants the learners to make further improvement, she must either explain to the learners how to make the sound, show the written form of the sound, or use some "trick", such as forcing, to help the learners make the correct sound (George, 1972). As well as giving a model for learners to copy, a teacher thus needs to be able to provide other help in teaching pronunciation.

Once the learners can make the sounds well the teacher can give a written model or show pictures or objects to get the learners to pronounce the sounds. Carr (1967) suggests that for a difficult sound the teacher should have a box containing objects that have the difficult sound as a part of their name. In this way quick practice can easily be given.

Difficult vowel sounds can often be made by using the exercises that Pike (1947) calls **slurring and bracketing**. In slurring, the tongue or another part of the mouth is slowly moved from one position to another. This is done several times with the learners copying the teacher. Then the movement is stopped a part of the way between the two sounds so that the wanted sound is produced. So, for example, the first sound is /ɪ/, and the last is /æ/. By stopping halfway, /e/ is produced. Bracketing is almost the same, except that the vowels are pronounced clearly and separately one after the other, for example, /ɪ æ/. The learner copies the teacher in order to do this. And then the learner tries to make the vowel halfway between the first two that were practised. The result will be /e/.

Diagrams for pronunciation involve a picture showing the position of the tongue and other parts of the mouth. Jones (1960) presents and describes these types of pictures in detail. A cut-out picture of the face may be used with the teacher's hand acting as the tongue. Often the front view of the mouth is useful, especially for vowels, /θ/ and /ð/, /f/ and /v/, /w/, etc.

In **testing the teacher**, some of the exercises that are used for hearing practice can be used to practise pronunciation. The learners take the teacher's place, and the teacher takes the learner's place. So, for the same-different exercise the learners individually pronounce pairs of words and the teacher says "the same" or "different".

Sometimes, **using the written forms** can help with new clusters. Learners can look at the structure of the syllable as a help for word recognition and vocabulary learning. The patterns for final consonant groups are much more complicated than the consonant groups at the beginning of the words. Here is a simple kind of exercise to get learners to find the main patterns at the beginning of words. This kind of exercise also shows the learners some of the connections between spelling and pronunciation.

Make a list of consonant groups at the beginning of these words. Note that qu is pronounced /kw/, and cr, cl, sch are pronounced /kr kl sk/.

through a place scale brown sky quality a crowd skill grass skin a train string break twice try straight spread trust fruit blow trousers travel blood brave pray a street twenty smile glory swim strange clever sleep fresh draw squeeze a crop steam trade blue splendid square quick glass stop a clock spring print smell drop scratch scarce throw proud dry frighten twelve split speed cry a queen scrape drink twins true a cloud bright brush small slow present strong green dress fly a spoon please black stone free a stick quite clean plan swam a school spell sweet grow clay a snake three close play quick grammar front bread glad

The learners can make patterns as a result of the listing and later the teacher can present nonsense words for the learners to decide if they are possible English words or not because of their patterns.

As well as having a group of sounds different from the group of sounds in other languages, English also puts these sounds together according to a certain system (Yasui, no date). For example, a word can begin with /sk/ but not with /ks/ and so on. Three-year-old native speakers seem to know this system. Most native speakers are able to recognise words which are *possible* English words according to the system, like /skæp/, or /tem/. They can also say which are not words according to the system, like /ksap/, or /letp/ (this skill has been used as a test of a person's reading ability). Words that are not made according to the system are often very difficult for native speakers to pronounce (Messer, 1967). Teaching learners of English the system or grammar of English sounds could have several good effects. It might be easier for learners to hear, pronounce, and remember new words because they fit in with patterns that the learners already know. Relating these patterns to spelling can have benefits for pronunciation.

Correcting Pronunciation Mistakes

When a learner makes a pronunciation mistake and the teacher wants to correct it quickly, the teacher can do any of the following things.

- The teacher repeats the word correctly several times with ordinary stress and intonation until the learner self-corrects by copying the teacher.
- The teacher repeats the word correctly giving extra stress and length to the part where the learner made the mistake.

- The teacher compares the mistake and the correct form: "Not lice but rice."
- The teacher writes the word on the blackboard correctly and underlines the part where the learner made a mistake. The teacher also says the word correctly.
- The teacher just says "No" and lets the learner find the mistake without help. The teacher can make a certain signal, like hitting the desk softly, when a learner makes a pronunciation mistake. This technique is used when the learners can make the correct sounds but forget to do so while talking.

Stress and Intonation

Languages can be classified according to whether they are stress-timed or syllable-timed. It used to be thought that in a stress-timed language (like English) the stresses were equal distances apart even though the number of syllables between each stress was not the same. This would mean that some syllables would have to be said very quickly if there were several between two stresses, and some would be said slowly if there were few between two stresses. In syllable-timed languages, the syllables occur at regular intervals (as in Spanish and Indonesian). Research indicates that the spacing of stresses is by no means equal in stress-timed languages although there is a tendency towards regularity (Dauer, 1983). The main differences between stress-timed and syllable-timed languages lie in syllable structure (syllable length varies more in stress-timed languages than in syllable-timed languages), vowel reduction (stress-timed languages are more likely to use centralised vowels in unstressed syllables and vowels may be shortened or omitted), and lexical stress (stress-timed languages usually have word level stress). When speakers of a syllable-timed language like Chinese or French learn English, they may need help in observing and copying the rhythmic patterns of speech. The following techniques may help. George (1990) very usefully discusses a range of features involved in the way different languages sound, and suggests gradual shaping to the wanted type. Aufderhaar (2004) found that getting learners to listen to and perform texts recorded by native speakers was viewed positively by some learners as a way of improving their control of pronunciation, particularly prosodic features. Some, however, felt it was rather time-consuming, although this objection could be dealt with by more careful class planning.

Teaching Word Stress

In English, one part of a word is usually said with greater strength, stress, than another part. Strong stress often goes with an increase in the length of the syllable and a change in intonation. There are no easy rules to find which syllable should be stressed in a word. The stress pattern of each word just has to be learned. A common mistake is to say words with the stress in the wrong place. Stress can be taught in the following ways.

- The teacher taps the stress pattern of a word, with a hard tap for the stressed syllables and soft for the others. The learners say the word.
- When the teacher provides a model she can make the stressed syllable longer than usual and the unstressed ones very short.
- When the learners say a word, they make a gesture to go with the stressed part of the word. This gesture can be a hand movement.
- The teacher says a sentence and she stops before a word that gives the learners problems with the stress. Instead of saying the word she taps the stress pattern on the table. The learners must guess the word by listening to the context and stress pattern, and then say it.

   "Very well, I'll come tap TAP tap tap." (immediately)

   If the learners need extra help to guess the word the first letter can be given.
- The learners are given a list of words. The teacher reads them and the learners underline the stressed syllables.
- The learners are given a list of words and they put them in groups according to their stress pattern. The teacher can give them some model words to represent each stress pattern. When practising stress the teacher can present words with the same stress pattern for practice.

Teaching Sentence Stress

The place of stress in an English sentence depends on the relative importance of the different words in the sentence. Usually nouns, adjectives, certain pronouns, main verbs and adverbs are given strong stress (Jones, 1960). Learners can be given practice in looking at the meaning of sentences to decide where the strong stress should be (Halverson, 1967). One sentence can be spoken in many different ways to give different meanings (Jones, 1960; Robinett, 1965). Allen (1972) suggests using a simple situation where a person is asking for something but the other person keeps giving him the wrong thing, "Give me a SMALL bottle of medicine." George and Neo (1974) point out the close relationship between stress and information distribution in a sentence, with the stressed parts conveying the least predictable information.

In English sentences the stressed syllables are roughly the same distance from each other. So, if there are many unstressed syllables between the stressed syllables, the unstressed syllables are said very quickly. A very common mistake, specially by speakers of Asian languages, is to make every syllable, stressed or unstressed, the same length. Learners can be helped to avoid this mistake in the following ways. When providing practice, it is important to give attention to the unstressed syllables as well as the stressed syllables. The unstressed syllables will be shorter and will probably contain a centralised vowel like /ə/. Weakening the unstressed syllables gives prominence to the stressed syllables.

It is worth checking that learners use weak forms of common words like *a, and, can, will, had, is, was,* and *not* in connected speech. For some learners it may also be necessary to practise leaving out sounds (elision) and assimilating adjacent sounds, to help keep the flow and rhythm of normal speech.

- The teacher taps the rhythms of sentences with his finger on the table. The learner practises saying the sentences while tapping in time with the teacher (Jones, 1960).
- The teacher explains the way rhythm works in an English sentence and gives models for the learners to copy.
- The teacher says a short sentence with two stresses and the learners repeat it. Then the sentence is built up in several steps into a long sentence that still has only two stresses and is repeated in almost the same length of time as the short sentence.
  The boy's in the house.
  The boy's in the old house.
  The little boy's in the old house.
  The little boy's not in the old house (Robinett, 1965).
- Reading poetry aloud can help to teach learners the rhythm of English sentences.

Teaching Intonation

Learners can practise intonation in the following ways.

- The learners can copy the teacher.
- The learners can make gestures to go with changes in intonation. The rise at the end of a Yes/No question can go with the speaker raising her eyebrows, or lifting a shoulder (Robinett, 1965).
- The learners say the last word of a sentence by itself with the correct intonation, rising or falling. Then word by word they build up the sentence from the end to the beginning while keeping the correct intonation (Robinett, 1965).
  "tea. or tea. coffee or tea. want coffee or tea. etc."
- The learners can be shown drawings of intonation patterns to help them understand what they should try to do.

Fitting Pronunciation into a Course

Several possibilities are available for making pronunciation improvement part of a course.

1. A special time is regularly set aside for direct attention to pronunciation for the whole class. Typical activities might include distinguishing sounds, identifying sounds, repetition drills, and monitored speaking activities.
2. Pronunciation is focused on occasionally, perhaps to set goals and activities for individual work.
3. Pronunciation errors are dealt with as they occur, usually on an individual level, or in a small group while others do other work.
4. Pronunciation is not given any special attention but meaning-focused speaking activities which can affect pronunciation are part of the listening and speaking programme. These activities might include split information activities, formal talks, poems and songs, read-and-look-up activities, and the blackboard reproduction exercise.

The type of attention given to pronunciation will depend partly on whether the teacher sees it as most useful to regard pronunciation as a skill to be developed through form-focused instruction using repetition and practice, or as a system of knowledge that evolves and develops with appropriate help through meaning-focused use.

Learners need practice in transferring what they have practised in controlled situations to unmonitored spontaneous use. Situations for speaking can be ranked on a continuum from careful and highly monitored to spontaneous. Table 5.1 shows such a range, starting from the most careful.

Learners can gradually move through the range of activities with a focus

Table 5.1 Types of Control and Techniques for Speaking

Degree and type of control	Techniques
Prepared reading aloud	Giving dictation Read and look up
Unprepared reading aloud	Chain story
Rehearsed formal speaking	4/3/2 Read and retell
Formal speaking with no time pressure	Peer talks
One-way information gap activities	Listen and do
Split information activities with time pressure	Find the difference Same or different

on bringing about change in particular sounds or aspects of pronunciation. In the careful activities, the learners prepare, monitor and receive feedback. In the spontaneous activities only feedback is provided.

It may also be useful for learners to have physical reminders to help them monitor a particular sound to bring about change. This physical reminder can be something like crossing your fingers before starting to speak to remind you to say /ð/ as correctly as possible.

The way correction and pronunciation practice is done can affect the learners' attitude to changing their own pronunciation. Stevick (1978) suggests three approaches to teaching pronunciation which take account of learners' feelings.

1. The teacher hardly speaks but guides the learners to find their own criteria for the sounds of the language. This is the approach followed in the Silent Way.
2. The pronunciation is given gently but clearly from a point outside of the learner's view but within their personal space. This often creates the illusion that what the learners hear is coming from inside their own heads. This is the approach followed in Community Language Learning.
3. The learners speak first, not the teacher. Then no matter whether the learners are right or wrong "the teacher gives the same word or phrase correctly, using a tone of voice that conveys interest and support, but which does not say 'right' or 'wrong' ". The student, in turn, may or may not repeat after the teacher. In this informative but non-evaluative atmosphere, students pick up most of what they need to know. The non-evaluative aspect of this technique reduces the alienation between student and teacher. Whatever information the students do not pick up in this way is provided from time to time by the teacher, in brief, matter-of-fact statements addressed to no-one in particular.

An effective way of showing learners the importance of an intelligible pronunciation is to get them to meet communication difficulties with peers (Jenkins, 2002). In his research on split information activities involving the re-labelling of diagrams, Newton (1995) found that at least 25 percent of the negotiation between learners focused on the spoken form of words. This resulted in the learners repeating the words, often with altered pronunciation, or spelling the words. It is not difficult for a teacher to design split information activities that focus on wanted sounds and increase the learners' awareness of the importance of pronunciation. Information gap activities involving the labelling of diagrams or plans are particularly useful.

Monitoring Pronunciation

The most effective way of testing a learner's pronunciation is to observe and record the learner performing in a variety of situations. This is not always possible and there have been ingenious suggestions to test groups of learners. For groups which are not too large learners can tape-record a passage using their best pronunciation. They are allowed to practise the passage as much as they like but they can only record it once (Whiteson, 1978). Another way that learners find enjoyable is for the teacher to hand out a sheet with minimal pair sentences on it (Hole, 1983). Here is an example of part of a sheet.

1. I asked him for a ship
                  a sheep
2. The pen is in my pocket
             pin
3. John was said to be going
             sad

The learners write their names at the top of the sheets. Then they draw a circle around one word in each minimal pair. They can choose any member of a pair of words. Then the teacher calls on the learners one by one to say each sentence containing the words they circled. The teacher writes which member of each pair they say. The learners' papers are collected and the teacher's notes are compared with what the learners circled.

Dobbyn (1976) devised a test for quite large groups. As in the test procedure devised by Hole (1983) the teacher does not know what the learners are trying to say. Ten different sheets are prepared, all based on the same minimal pairs. Here are three such pairs.

1(a) She couldn't be heard in class.
 (b) She couldn't be hard in class.
2(a) He guards his gin carefully.
 (b) He guards his shin carefully.
3(a) Give him his tie back.
 (b) Give him his toy back.

One of the ten sheets will contain these sentences and the key.

1. She couldn't be heard in class.
2. He guards his shin carefully.
3. Give him his tie back.
   1a, 2b, 3a

Another sheet may have these sentences and the key.

1. She couldn't be heard in class.
2. He guards his chin carefully.
3. Give him his tie back.
   1a, 2a, 3a

The sheets are distributed so that the teacher does not know who has which sheet. As each learner is called on to pronounce the sentences on their sheet, the teacher writes a or b under their name for each number. Then the teacher gets the learner to read the key aloud and the teacher marks what they wrote.

It is useful to see improvement in pronunciation as fitting into the four strands of a course. An intelligible pronunciation can be encouraged by meaning-focused input and meaning-focused output during communication activities where learners with different first languages are trying to get their meaning across (Jenkins, 2002). Pronunciation can also be helped through a deliberate focus on individual sounds, consonant clusters, and supra-segmentals. Fluency activities may also have a role to play in the improvement of pronunciation. Because fluency and accuracy affect each other, working on very easy tasks to improve fluency may also have a positive effect on pronunciation accuracy, although this remains to be researched.

The intelligibility of a speaker's pronunciation is also dependent on the attitude of the listener. If the listener wants to understand, is sympathetic to the speaker, and makes an effort to understand, intelligibility will be greater. Pronunciation practice can take learners so far, but communication is a two-way process and some responsibility for understanding also lies with the listener.

CHAPTER 6

Learning through Task-focused Interaction

This chapter examines activities that bring listening and speaking together in communicative activities. This integration of listening and speaking emphasises active listening with the listener negotiating and shaping the spoken message. Part of the skill of listening is learning how to take an active role in providing feedback to the speaker (Brown, 1986). This feedback may involve pointing out problems with the comprehensibility of the message and specifying where the problem lies. This feedback and questioning is called *negotiation*. Here is an example of a group of learners negotiating successfully with each other during a speaking task.

L3   ... "All enclosures should be filled" (reading from task sheet).
L2   "Enclosures should be filled". *Enclosure,* do you know?
L1   What means *enclosure?* Do you know?
L3   Close ah,—"should be filled".
L2   No I don't know enclos- enclosed.
L1   *Filled* what means *fill?* Oh oh all enclosed, I think that all enclosed that means enclosed.
L2   Fill.
L3   Filled, filled.
L2   Ohh.
L1   Every every area yes should be filled.
L2   Should be filled.
L3   Should be put put something inside.

L1 Yes because yes yes because you know two? the-
L2 I see. No empty rooms ahh.
L3 No empty rooms yeah.
L2 Two is the empty I see.
L1 Yeah empty so we must fill it, okay?

One of the main ways that negotiation helps the listener learn is by clarifying unknown items. As Michael Long (1996) claims,

> . . . tasks that stimulate negotiation for meaning may turn out to be one among several useful language-learning situations, in or out of classrooms, for they may be one of the easiest ways to facilitate a learner's focus on form without losing sight of a lesson's (or conversation's) predominant focus on meaning.
>
> (p. 454)

Negotiation also plays other roles in assisting language development, such as the following which are based on Long's detailed discussion of interaction (Long, 1996: 445–454). Negotiation:

- makes input understandable without simplifying it, so that learnable language features are retained
- breaks the input into smaller digestible pieces
- raises awareness of formal features of the input
- gives learners opportunities for direct learning of new forms
- provides a "scaffold" within which learners can produce increasingly complex utterances
- pushes learners to express themselves more clearly and precisely— "pushed output"
- makes learners more sensitive to their need to be comprehensible.

Overall, interaction helps language learning by providing opportunities to learn from others, often through negotiation, and by speakers having to adjust their output to communicate with others. This interaction helps learning by providing plenty of comprehensible input, by encouraging pushed output, by making learners aware of what they do not know, and by helping learners develop the language and strategies needed for interaction. Susan Gass sums up the value of negotiation in the following way:

> The claim is not that negotiation causes learning nor that there is a theory of learning based on interaction. Rather, negotiation is a facilitator of learning; it is one means but not the only means of drawing attention to areas of needed change. It is one means by which input can become comprehensible and manageable, [and] . . .

it is a form of negative evidence [helping] learners to recognize the inadequacy of their own rule system.

(Gass, 1997: 131–132)

Encouraging Negotiation

Most of the techniques in this chapter encourage negotiation. The extent to which negotiation helps language learning depends on what is negotiated and how far the negotiation takes the learner through *comprehending*, *noticing, comparing* and *using* unfamiliar or partly unfamiliar language items.

Several studies of negotiation have shown the range of reasons for negotiation (Aston, 1986; Larsen-Freeman and Long, 1991). These include keeping the group together by "celebrating agreement", clarifying poorly presented items, clarifying because of inattention, clarifying unknown items, and clarifying the task procedure. Only a few of these are likely to contribute directly to language learning. When the teacher monitors tasks involving negotiation to judge their effectiveness, the teacher should look carefully for negotiation of lexical and grammatical items and should notice whether form or meaning is being negotiated. Direct training of speaking strategies can have a positive effect on learners' development of speaking skills (Sayer, 2005). Training can involve: (1) explanation of discourse strategies like "holding the floor", negotiating meaning, providing feedback to the speaker, and managing turn-taking; (2) observing conversations using a checklist and later providing feedback; and (3) learners transcribing recordings of their own speech and critiquing them.

Using Written Input to Encourage Negotiation

Newton's (1995) research on the effect of written input on negotiation showed that in the tasks he used, *all* of the negotiated vocabulary was in the written input sheets used in the activity. That is, the learners did not negotiate vocabulary that they incidentally brought into the activity. If this finding is true across a variety of activities and texts, it means that by careful choice or rewriting of texts, teachers can set up wanted vocabulary to be negotiated (Joe, Nation and Newton, 1996; Nation, 2001: 134–143).

Let us take the **agony column** activity as an example. In some newspapers there is a place for letters from readers to be printed. Readers write in describing their relationship problems or other personal problems and an answer giving advice about their problems is printed next to each letter. These letters and their answers can be used for class discussion. Hall (1971) suggests these steps.

1. Read the letter to the learners, but not the answer. Unknown vocabulary and other difficulties should be explained. The learners can take notes as they listen to the letter, ask questions, repeat it aloud phrase by phrase, or write it as dictation.
2. After the letter is read, the learners discuss it in small groups and suggest advice of their own.
3. The last step is when the teacher presents the advice given in the newspaper. This advice can be discussed and compared with the advice suggested by the learners.

In order to encourage negotiation, in step 1 the learners are simply given the written version of the letter. Before doing this the teacher checks that the letter contains about six to eight items that may be beyond most of the learners' present level but which are appropriate for them to learn. The teacher may wish to simplify the other vocabulary which is not worth spending time on. There is nothing wrong with adapting the text providing the teacher is confident that adaptations represent normal language use. Step 3, the comparison of the group's advice with that provided by the newspaper, will provide a useful repetition of the items.

Here is a typical letter. The underlined vocabulary is in the Academic Word List (Coxhead, 2000) and is the learning goal of the activity.

Dear Belle,

My boss keeps inviting me to <u>participate</u> in various sporting activities with him, such as playing golf and squash. I am quite good at the sports and enjoy them. However, it is <u>affecting</u> my relationship with my wife. The time that we would usually spend together is now <u>devoted</u> to keeping my boss happy. I don't know what decision to make. Should I refuse my boss and risk my promotion, or should I continue with golf and squash and risk my marriage?

Confused sportsman

There are many techniques which provide written input which could encourage negotiation. These include **completion activities, ordering activities, split information activities, ranking, problem solving,** and **modify the statements**, and are described later in this chapter.

Seedhouse (1999) notes that it is the nature of the task that determines the kind of language use that occurs. Coughlan and Duff (1994) provide evidence, however, that it is the learners who determine what kind of interaction occurs with a given task (see also Nakahama, Tyler and van Lier, 2001). In addition, strongly focused two-way tasks can result in the use of almost telegraphic language because this is the most efficient way of getting the message across, particularly when there is a time limit placed on the task. Similarly, the way in which the learners take turns in a task is largely determined by the nature of the task. Teachers need to monitor tasks well and use this feedback to redesign tasks to suit learning goals.

Using Information Distribution to Encourage Negotiation

It is possible to distinguish four kinds of group work according to the way the information needed in the activity is distributed among the learners (Nation, 1989b). These four ways are:

1. All learners have the same information (a cooperating arrangement).
2. Each learner has different essential information (a split information arrangement) (Nation, 1977).
3. One learner has all the information that the others need (a superior-inferior arrangement).
4. The learners all see the same information but each one has a different task.

The term "information gap activities" is sometimes used in the literature. These can include split information tasks and superior-inferior tasks. The term information gap will be largely avoided here to preserve the distinction between these two kinds of tasks.

The first two types of information distribution are the ones that most encourage negotiation, and there has been considerable research into their effects. **Split information activities** have been called two-way tasks, or jigsaw tasks, and cooperating tasks have been called one-way tasks. The clearest example of a split information task can be seen when the learners work in pairs. In each pair, one learner (A) has a sheet of paper with 30 simple numbered pictures on it (see Figure 6.1 below). The other learner in the pair (B) has a similar sheet except that about half of their pictures are the same as Learner A's and the other half are not the same as Learner A's.

Learners A and B sit facing each other. They must not be able to see the information on each other's sheet. Because there is a cross next to item 1 on their sheet, Learner A begins by describing the first picture. Learner B listens carefully to this description, asks Learner A any questions that they need to, and looks at the first picture on their sheet to decide whether or not their picture is exactly the same as Learner A's. If Learner B thinks it is the same, they say "the same" to Learner A and they both write **S** next to item 1 on their sheets. If, after listening to the description given by Learner A, Learner B thinks their picture is different, they say "different" and both learners write **D** next to item 1 on their sheets. When the first item has been completed, Learner B begins describing item 2 because there is a cross

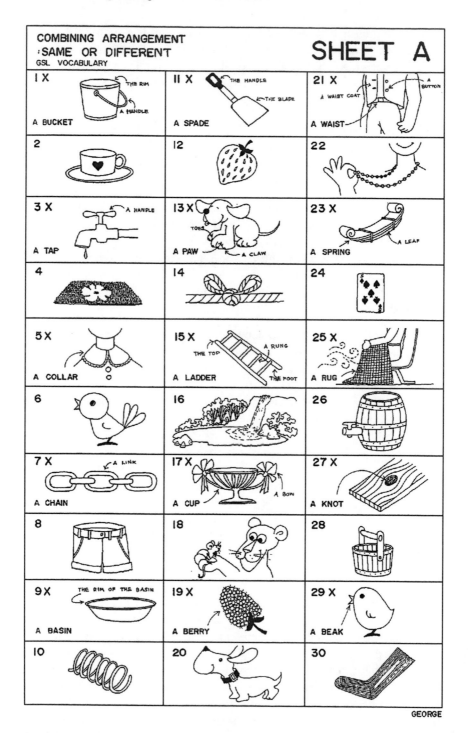

Figure 6.1 A Split Information Activity

GEORGE,

next to item 2 on their sheet. Each pair works through the items in this way. After five or ten items have been completed the learners change partners. When all the items have been completed, learners A and B in each pair put their two sheets next to each other and compare the pictures to see if their answers were correct.

The essential feature of the split information arrangement is that only by working together in combining their material can the learners find the required answers. A learner cannot find the answer simply by looking at their own material.

Split information tasks can be used with learners at any level, from beginners to advanced students, if appropriate materials are employed (Nation, 1977). One weakness of these tasks when they require labelling and completion of diagrams with words is that learners can resort to spelling out words to each other and in so doing reduce the quality of meaning-focused talk.

Cooperating tasks involve all the learners having the same information. For example, in a **ranking** task, the learners are given a list of items and a criterion for ranking or choosing amongst the items. They must arrange the items according to the criterion or choose the top 3 and the bottom 1 (Green, 1975; Thomas and Nation, 1979). Here is an example.

You are alone and lost in the jungle; put the following things in order of importance for your survival.

a sleeping bag
a radio (for listening only)
an axe
a gun and ten bullets
matches
a tent
a torch
a map of the area
a cooking pot
three cans of food
three metres of rope
a story book

This type of problem-solving activity can be done by moving through a variety of group sizes. First, the learners are presented with the problem and are then asked to think individually about the problem and choose a possible solution. In the second step, the learners work in small groups to reach an agreement. The third step involves whole-class work in which groups compare their rankings and the teacher facilitates discussion of the rankings and of language issues that came up in the task. Activities like ranking with a strong focus on reaching consensus can encourage negotiation of language items. If you want to reach agreement, then there must be understanding. Here are some techniques that require a consensus.

In **modify the statements**, the learners are given a set of controversial statements, such as "Every child needs at least one brother and sister". They work in groups to make changes to the statements so that everybody in the group can agree with them (Gower, 1981).

In the following kind of **problem solving**, the learners are given a problem to solve. They must do this by reaching an agreement amongst themselves. They should not do this by voting but by discussion. The work is done in small groups of about six people. When they have reached an agreement they report the result of their discussion to the class. Here is an example from Cole (1972).

A teacher sees a student cheating in an examination. He is the student who produces the student newspaper. He is a good student, but because of his outside work his marks have not been very high. If he gets to law school he will probably become a very great lawyer. What should the teacher do?

1   Pretend not to see the cheating.
2   Quietly ask him to stop cheating.
3   Tell the class that someone has been cheating and if it happens again that person will be sent out.
4   Send the student out of the room and tell the class the reason.
5   Do the same as (4) but also tell the head of the school so that the student is forced to leave the school.

The learners must choose one of the five possibilities.

In **complete the map** each learner has an incomplete version of a map or diagram and each learner has information that the other(s) do not have. By combining this information each learner can make a complete map. They do this by keeping their map hidden from the others and by describing what is on their map for the others to draw on theirs.

In the **strip story** the teacher chooses a story that has roughly as many sentences as there are learners in the group. The teacher writes each sentence from the story on different pieces of paper. The story should be one that the learners have not met before. It should contain known vocabulary and sentence patterns. Each learner is given a different sentence from the story to memorise. If there are not enough sentences for each learner to have one it does not matter, because they can still participate in ordering the sentences. If there are more sentences than learners, then some learners can have two short sentences to memorise. So, each learner sees only one sentence and does not see the other sentences in the story. After each learner has memorised their sentence, the pieces of paper with the sentences on them are collected by the teacher. Then each learner tells their sentence to the others in the group and without doing any writing at all the learners arrange themselves to solve the problem of putting the sentences in the right order to tell the story (Gibson, 1975). The teacher takes no part in the activity. The technique allows the learners to communicate in the foreign language with each other to solve the problem. The solving of the problem is less important than the communication that needs to take place in order to solve the problem.

In a beginners class this activity can provide an excellent way of practising key phrases related to the students' lives that have been previously learnt in class. For instance, the following recount was generated by learners in a class of older, retired, absolute beginners in an ESL context:

> In the morning I get up at 7 o'clock. I have a shower and eat my breakfast. After breakfast, I do the dishes. I leave home at 8 o'clock and catch the bus to class. In the evening, my jobs are to help cook dinner and do the dishes. After dinner, I watch TV. I go to bed at about 11 o'clock.

This provided the basis for a strip story activity. The learners had to order themselves in a line according to the sentence that each had memorised, and then retell the recount in sequence. Similarly, the strip story activity can be used with short, set dialogues that learners have been learning.

Factors Affecting the Amount and Type of Negotiation

Several factors affect the amount, type and effect of negotiation.

1. Pair work usually produces more negotiations on the same task than work in a group of four (Fotos and Ellis, 1991).
2. Cooperating tasks produce more negotiation of the meaning of vocabulary than information gap tasks (Newton, 1995). Information gap tasks produce a lot of negotiation but not all of it is negotiation of word meaning or indeed language features.
3. The signals learners make affects the adjustment of output during a task. In a study of output in activities involving native speakers working with non-native speakers, Pica, Holliday, Lewis and Morgenthaler (1989) found that the most important factor determining whether learners adjusted their output was the type of signal made by their partner. When their partner asked for clarification (What? I still don't know what the word is.), the learners were more likely to adjust what they said, than if their partner asked for confirmation by

repeating what the learner had just said, by changing it (**NNS** house has three windows? **NS** three windows?), or by completing or elaborating it (**NNS** there is a car parking . . . left side **NS** of the picture, right?). The researchers caution, however, that confirmation checks that do not lead to adjusted output may still have an important role to play in language acquisition in that they provide models for input.

Using Learner Training to Encourage Negotiation

In order to negotiate, learners need to know the language features needed for negotiation and to develop negotiation strategies. Anderson and Lynch (1988) have reviewed studies with young native speakers on the effect of training on the use of negotiation while listening. The training can involve telling learners the importance of asking for more information, watching others ask, and providing simple plans of what to do when there is a comprehension problem. Anderson and Lynch conclude: "The successful methods [of training young native speakers] seem to depend on the listener already possessing the requisite skills, but not realising their relevance to the current listening task" (p. 30). Encouraging second language learners to negotiate can involve learning the appropriate language items and procedures to negotiate and providing opportunities for practice. If these steps are not successful, the simple training procedures described above may be useful.

When taking part in a conversation, a learner may find that there are unknown words or structures, or that what the speaker said was not clear. If this happens, one strategy is to ask for clarification. The simplest language needed to do this includes phrases like "Pardon?", "What?", or even more colloquially "Eh?". Another possibility is to repeat the part just before the unclear part and add "what", as in "He what?", or "He agreed what?". These phrases can usefully be taught before learners do activities like the following, in order to practise the phrases and the strategy.

Clennell (1999) describes a useful procedure for making learners aware of the linguistic and socio-linguistic features of interactive spoken language. Stage 1 involves preparing for an interview and then carrying out the interview. The preparation can involve focusing on appropriate ways of addressing the interviewee, different ways of requesting an interview, and so on. It can also involve ways of managing the discourse by asking the interviewee to repeat or slow down. Stage 2 involves transcribing the recorded interview and coming to an understanding of what happened during the interview. Stage 3 involves presenting the analysed transcription to the class in the form of a seminar presentation with accompanying discussion. Lynch (2001) found plenty of evidence that transcribing their own spoken interaction resulted in learners finding plenty to improve and being able to make substantial corrections to the language of the transcription. There was also a useful follow-up role for the teacher in providing helpful corrective feedback especially in vocabulary choice. Mennim (2003) found that the teacher's feedback on learners' written transcription of a taped rehearsal of a presentation had substantial positive effects on the grammatical accuracy of a subsequent presentation.

Listen and do activities can also give rise to negotiation if they are at the right level of difficulty. Picture drawing in pairs has often been used in research on interaction and negotiation (see, for example, Mackey, 1999). For example:

> "Draw a circle. Draw a cross in the circle. Draw a line under the circle. Draw a square around the circle . . ." or "Draw a circle. This will be a person's face. Draw an ear on each side. The left ear is bigger than the right ear . . ."

Sometimes communication is difficult because the speaker is going too fast or is not being considerate of the listener. If this happens, the learner can try to control the speaker. The language needed to do this consists of phrases like "Please speak more slowly" and "Could you say that again?"

In the **controlling the teacher** technique learners gain control of the listening material. When the learners have this control, listening exercises can become learning exercises. The teacher makes sure that the learners know the following sentences and, if necessary, writes them on the blackboard so that they can be seen during the exercise.

> Please say the last word (sentence/paragraph) again.
> Excuse me, please speak more slowly.
> Excuse me, what was the word in front of <u>king</u>?
> Could you tell me the meaning of <u>convince</u>?
> Excuse me, how do you spell <u>apply</u>?

Then, he tells the learners that he is going to read a text aloud for them to listen to. He tells them that after they listen to the text he will check their answers to some questions about the text. The teacher gives the learners copies of the questions or writes the questions on the blackboard. He also tells the learners that at any time during the reading of the text they can ask him to stop, read more slowly, repeat, go back to the beginning, spell a word, explain the meaning of a word, or read more quickly. Then, the learners look at the questions and listen. However, the teacher deliberately reads the first two sentences of the text too quickly for the learners to follow. Then, he stops and looks at the learners for instruction. He does not do anything further until the learners give him instructions. When the teacher finally reaches the end of the text and the learners have no further instructions for him, he asks the learners for the answers to the questions. As an alternative to questions, the teacher can divide the text in two and make copies. The learners then work in pairs, each reading their part of the text while the other learner interrupts with clarification questions as required.

Could you repeat that? (Folse, 1991) involves a learner or group of learners dictating to someone writing on the blackboard, while they are facing the other way. Therefore, the people dictating cannot see what is being written on the blackboard. This can be done with two teams and similar but not the same sentences.

Discover the answer is another technique to encourage learners to question the speaker.

The teacher asks the learners a question that she is sure that they cannot answer, for example,

"How many kilometres is it from here to Paris?"

When one learner tries to guess the answer the teacher says things like

"No, it's less than that." or
"No, it's less than half of that." or
"Take away a few kilometres." etc.

By the things that she says the teacher guides the learners to the correct answer. This is an amusing technique because at last by listening to what the teacher says about the answers the learners are able to give the correct answer to the question although they really did not know the answer before. The technique helps learn the phrases like "more than that" which guide learners towards the answer.

In **discover the story** one learner has a copy of a story. They tell the topic of the story to others in the group and they ask questions to discover what the story is about. There are many variations of this technique (Joycey, 1982). The passage can be a story written by the learner and the information given to the other learners, instead of being the topic, can be some important words of the story.

All of these activities increase the need for negotiation between the learners in a group. They all involve an information gap which may be there because of split information or a superior-inferior information distribution.

Monitoring Negotiation

Group work can have a variety of learning goals and monitoring should reflect these goals. If the goal is the learning of language items, then the amount of support that learners provide each other during the activity will be of major interest. This support can take the form of negotiating the meaning of language items, the encouragement of turn-taking to involve all of the group in the activity, the valuing of contributions by commenting positively on or picking up others' ideas, and the modelling and supplying of needed items.

Teachers or learners acting as observers can look for these kinds of support and comment on them to the group as a way of bringing about the development of group support skills that will help language learning.

If observation shows that there is a need for increased support, there are several ways of arranging this.

1. Parts of group work sessions are recorded and used as case studies to show learners how to increase support.
2. Each learner in the group is assigned a different role to play during a group work activity. Thus, one person could have the role of encouraging each person to contribute to the discussion. Another person could have the role of commenting positively on good ideas put forward by others, and so on.
3. The teacher should consider redesigning the activity to include an information gap, a series of well-defined steps for the learners to follow, or a different outcome such as ranking, completion, or distinguishing.
4. It may be necessary to rearrange the assignment of learners to groups so that, for example, learners of a similar proficiency level are in the same group, or so that there is not a gender mix.

As well as monitoring the dynamics of group work, it is also useful to monitor learners' focus on the task. This monitoring can involve looking at the amount of discussion of how to do the task, the amount of time spent focused on the task, and the amount of use of language items from the written input used in the task.

Learning through Non-negotiated Interaction

Although negotiation is a very effective means of encouraging learning through interaction, it does not account for most of the learning through interaction. Most learning will occur through guessing from context which is not overtly signalled, and by the non-negotiated noticing of language features (Newton, 1995; Nation, 2001: 123–125). Sometimes there may be overt signs of this noticing. In his study of units of oral expression, Bygate (1988: 74–75) provides examples of how "the flexibility of oral discourse can make it easier for the learner to pick up a lexical item or structure offered by a colleague . . . before proceeding to weave it into a phrase or clause".

S9:	on yours you have a clock and I have a
S10:	a picture
S9:	a picture (p. 73)

S3:	I think there are more than three differences
S1:	yes
S2:	yes
S1:	more than three differences (p. 70)

Small group activities provide an opportunity for the productive use of items supported by the interaction with colleagues. It is likely that the design features to encourage this production include the use of information gap tasks which contain a large amount of shared information.

The **find the differences** activity is a good example of this. In this activity a pair of learners have a similar picture each, but they have to find the differences by describing and not showing their pictures to each other. In this activity the support comes from the common features of the two pictures. Support may also involve some kind of support during the task such as notes, pictures with annotations, or objects. Breitkreuz (1972) suggests a sequence of speaking activities starting with a set of pictures. The learners are shown several pictures that tell a story. Usually there are about four pictures. First, the learners must describe the pictures and tell the story in their own words. Then they retell the story as a dialogue. After this they can act it. Questions can be used to help the learners. The pictures can be taken from books of picture stories or joke books, or they can be made of stick drawings drawn by the teacher.

In this procedure the teacher may simply rely on group cooperation to produce the wanted vocabulary and constructions. If monitoring the activity shows that this does not happen, then it may be necessary for the teacher to write words and phrases on the pictures for the learners to use. This gives the first activity something of a focus on form, and so the follow-up activities of turning it into a dialogue and then acting it may serve to bring back the meaning focus. Fowles (1970) suggests using humorous cartoons in a similar way. This has the learning goals of cultural understanding and language development.

All these kinds of support allow learners to draw on explicit knowledge of the language in their spoken production.

Monitoring Learners Beginning to Speak

Some learners may be reluctant to speak. It is important to find out the causes for this and to deal with the causes. The following table outlines some possibilities.

Table 6.1 Causes and Solutions for Learners who are Reluctant to Speak

Possible causes	Way of checking the cause	Solutions
Inadequate vocabulary	Use the 1000 level test (see Nation, 2001).	Use activities where the learner can study the vocabulary beforehand.
Inadequate control of grammar	Use sentence completion tests to see areas of strength and weakness.	Use controlled activities like **substitution tables** and **What is it?** Use guided or creative techniques to develop control of grammar.
Lack of fluency	Provide a long "wait time" to see if the learner is able to construct a spoken sentence.	Do repetitive activities like **4/3/2**.
Shyness	Compare how the learner talks to the teacher with how the learner talks to peers.	Start the learner with safe, small group activities, gradually increasing the risk.
Lack of encouragement	See if the learner will speak with friends in English in the playground or in pair activities.	Work in a small group with the learner giving a lot of encouragement (Day, 1981).

Each of the possible causes for reluctance to speak is accompanied by a way of checking the cause. A vocabulary of 1000 words is easily enough for substantial spoken production. Where learners have a very small vocabulary, very controlled activities may need to be used.

It is important to be aware that reluctance to speak may not be only because of language difficulties. Day (1981) found that some learners possessed adequate language skills, but had not received enough encouragement to speak in a classroom. When they were taken out of the classroom for short periods of time with one or two other learners and given lots of encouragement to speak, they were soon speaking a lot. After several sessions of such speaking, they seemed more willing to contribute to speaking in the larger class.

Observing learners in speaking activities can provide important information for the teacher about the learners' control of developmental features, like question making, and other features. This information can indicate to the teacher where language-focused instruction could usefully be directed. The presence of a feature in the learners' speaking is a sign that formal teaching could have a positive effect on expanding and refining its use (Pienemann, 2003).

CHAPTER 7

Learning through Pushed Output

The comprehension approach suggests that speaking should not be encouraged until learners have substantial receptive experience and knowledge of the language system. Some researchers, however, argue that the knowledge that is needed to speak will not come unless the learners are "pushed" to speak. Swain (2005) argues that learners can comprehend input without having to look closely at the grammar. If, however, they are "pushed" to produce output, then the attention that they give to the grammar changes. The idea behind pushed output is that knowledge of the L2 does not transfer automatically from reception to production. Comprehension processes involve semantic decoding. Production also involves syntactic processing. Biber's (1989) research on the various clusters of syntactic items in different text types suggests that learners might be made aware of gaps in their productive knowledge of language features if they are required to speak in unfamiliar genres. The aim of setting demanding tasks, then, is to encourage learners to extend their use of grammatical features and words. There are other ways of making tasks demanding, including getting learners to talk on unfamiliar topics, speaking where high standards of performance are expected, speaking without the opportunity for planning or preparation, and speaking in formal situations without the interactive support of others.

Learners are "pushed" when, through encouragement or necessity, they have to produce spoken language in unfamiliar areas. These areas may be unfamiliar because the learners are more used to listening than speaking, or are not accustomed to speaking certain kinds of discourse, or are now expected to produce a higher standard of spoken language in terms of accuracy, precision, coherence and appropriateness. Pushed output extends speakers and in doing so heightens their awareness of the importance of particular grammatical features in productive use of the language.

Without pushed output learners mainly acquire language features that are necessary for comprehension. Givon, Yang and Gernsbacher (1990) argue that because language learners can only give their attention to one demanding task at a time, they initially learn vocabulary. Once vocabulary recognition is largely automated, they can then give their attention to grammar. Swain suggests that if learners are not pushed to produce output, then there is little reason for them to pay attention to the grammar needed for production. Pushed output can result in the learner moving "from a purely semantic analysis of the language to a syntactic analysis of it" (1985: 252). This analysis could result in the learning of new grammar or in making "fuzzy" grammar more precise.

Pushed output does not mean that learners have to be pushed to produce as soon as an item is introduced. There is value in building up receptive experience, but this needs to be seen as only a first step. Learners need to be pushed to turn their receptive knowledge into productive use.

Pushing Output

When planning for a variety of speaking tasks to push learners' output there are several factors to consider. These include covering a range of topics, a range of text types, and a range of performance conditions.

Topic

Learners should be pushed to speak on a range of topics. Van Ek and Alexander (1980) provide a categorisation of topics. West (1960: 113–134), in his classification of the Minimum Adequate Vocabulary, also provides a range of possible topic areas. Topic is most likely to have an effect on the vocabulary that is used as each topic is likely to have its particular technical, topic-related vocabulary. Covering a good range of topics in a course ensures that a wide range of vocabulary is used. Topic will also have a relationship with amount of background knowledge, as learners may be familiar with the content of some topics and not with others. There could be strong gender difference effects in relation to background knowledge of topics which can make some topics much more demanding than others for male and female learners.

Text Type

Biber (1989) distinguished eight major spoken and written text types on the basis of the clustering of largely grammatical features. These text types included intimate interpersonal interaction, "scientific" exposition, imaginative narrative and involved persuasion. Although most of these were written types, many of them do have spoken equivalents. The most useful distinctions to consider when ensuring that learners are pushed to cope with a range of text types are:

1. Involved interaction versus monologue. Is only one person speaking or are speakers interacting with each other?
2. Colloquial speech versus formal speech.
3. Short turns versus long turns. Do speakers make short contributions to a conversation or is there opportunity for longer largely uninterrupted speech?
4. Interactional versus transactional speech. Is the goal of the speaking to establish a friendly relationship or is it to convey important information (Brown, 1981)?
5. Narrative versus non-narrative.

Learners should have the opportunity to speak across the range of these types of speaking.

Performance Conditions

When learners perform speaking tasks they can do this under a variety of conditions. One set that has received a reasonable amount of attention in research is the opportunity for planning before speaking.

Planning

Planning involves preparing for a task before the task is performed. Typically it involves having time to think about a given topic, having time to prepare what to say, and taking brief notes about what to say. The task may involve being given a set of pictures that represent a story to talk about, describing a LEGO model, preparing a small lecture, making a decision, or providing personal information (Ortega, 1999).

Planning helps language production because it allows part of the work to be done before the task so that there are less things to attend to while the task is being performed. In research studies it has been found that about ten minutes' planning time is usually enough to give good results. The effects of planning are usually measured by looking at the effects on fluency, grammatical complexity, and grammatical accuracy. In several studies, planning had positive effects on fluency and grammatical complexity, but had mixed effects on accuracy.

Getting learners to use new language items while their attention is focused on the meaning that they are conveying is a challenging part of activity design. One of the most effective ways of bringing receptive language knowledge into productive use is to make use of techniques which involve **retelling**. This retelling may be retelling of a written text or of spoken input. Here is part of a retelling of a text (Joe, 1998).

The written input
One of the greatest human problems is <u>chronic</u> pain—continuing, often <u>severe</u> pain caused by such disorders as lower-back problems and cancer. Chronic pain is so severe that people are incapacitated by it.

The retelling
The <u>chronic</u> pain . . . I don't understand exactly what mean . . . what is it. But I think it is a <u>severe</u> pain very: severe: . . . disease it . . . always happened when: the human have . . . <u>severe</u> pain at . . . the back in the lower part of the back . . . or cancer . . . something like that—it make people strengthen less.

In this particular example, the learner was tested on the underlined vocabulary some days before and the test indicated that these items were unknown. However, the retelling task pushed the learner to make sense of the items from the input and to use them productively. Clearly there is a variety of ways in which the items could be used, ranging from an exact repetition of the input context to very creative use resulting from generalisations based on analogy.

Giving learners a chance to prepare for tasks can increase their chances of success. Such preparation could involve the **retelling** of a previously studied written text (Joe, 1998) as described above, group members helping in preparation and rehearsal before the task, or research and planning on an assigned topic. In **class judgement**, preparation is an essential part of the task. Two learners are chosen to be the competitors in a quiz. They are given a text to read which they will later be quizzed on. The rest of the class also have the text and the questions which the competitors will be asked. The competitors do not see the questions. Then the competitors are asked the questions orally and the rest of the class note whether they think the answers are right or wrong (Picken, 1988).

In an **ask and answer** activity (Simcock, 1993), the learners work in pairs. One learner has a text to study and the other has a set of questions based on the text. The learners may work together on the text. Then one learner questions the other to get them to display their knowledge of the text. They practice this for a few times and eventually do it in front of the class. The performance is done without looking at the text. Many variations of this technique are possible, particularly in the relationship of the questions to the text and the type of processing required to answer them.

Time Pressure

The second major performance condition affecting speaking is time pressure. Recently researchers have distinguished on-line planning and pre-talk planning (Yuan and Ellis, 2003). On-line planning involves paying careful attention to turning ideas into speech while they speak, and this is more likely to have a positive effect on accuracy. On-line planning is helped by having plenty of time to speak. Pre-task planning, as in **prepared talks**, is more likely to allow learners to focus on the range of ideas to cover and the organisation of these ideas. Giving learners plenty of time to perform a speaking task allows them to access both their implicit and explicit grammatical knowledge and thus increase the quality of their spoken output.

Amount of Support

Supported or guided tasks allow learners to operate under the most favourable conditions for production. An important design feature in such tasks is the presence of patient, understanding, sympathetic and supportive listeners. There are several ways to achieve this. One way is to train the listeners in supportive listening strategies. These can include providing plenty of wait time while the speaker prepares what to say, using the **you said ...** strategy to periodically summarise what the speaker has said, asking easy questions to direct the speaker as in the **ask and answer** activity described above (Simcock, 1993) and, after sufficient wait time, supplying needed phrases and vocabulary if the speaker is struggling. An important requirement in supportive listening is giving the speaker the chance to find the language items needed without being overwhelmed by support. Using three learners in a speaking activity can be a useful way of training supportive listeners. One learner is the speaker, one is the supportive listener, and one is monitoring the supportive listener with a checklist.

Checklist for monitoring supportive listening

- Did the listener wait long enough before giving help?
- Did the listener provide positive comments on well produced sentences?
- Did the listener provide useful words and phrases?
- Did the listener keep the main focus on the message?

The three discuss the monitor's findings at the end of the speaking task. Another way to get supportive listening is to give listeners the chance to experience the difficulties of speaking and to reflect on these difficulties.

Standard of Performance

The fourth major performance condition affecting speaking is the standard of output expected. The pressure on learners to perform well is increased if they have to speak in public, and if they are aware that some judgement is going to be made on their performance. Doing transactional speaking with others when important information has to be conveyed and where it needs to be conveyed accurately is also a way of pushing output. Speaking with others can be supportive, it can also be demanding.

Let us now look briefly at how learners can be helped in informal speaking before looking in more detail at formal speaking.

Informal Speaking

Informal speaking typically involves tasks where conveying information is not as important as maintaining friendly relationships. Brown (1978) calls this interactional speaking as opposed to transactional speaking. Interactional speaking can be supported in the following ways. This support enables learners to produce what they would not normally be able to produce.

1. Learners can be taught conversational strategies that can help keep the conversation going (Holmes and Brown, 1976). A very useful technique for doing that is called **Q–>SA+EI**. What this formula means is a question (Q) should be followed by a short answer (SA) and then some extra information about the answer (EI). So if someone asks "How long have you been here?", the reply may be "About six months, but I found it very difficult at first". This extra information then provides an opportunity for the person asking the question to continue the conversation, typically by taking up the point raised in the extra information, "What were the difficulties you had?". This very useful strategy deserves quite a lot of practice in class, particularly in guiding learners in the kinds of extra information that they can provide. It is also a good way for the person being questioned to take control of an interview or conversation by using the extra information to guide the direction of the conversation (Nation, 1980).
2. Having a supportive partner in a conversation can make speaking much easier. Learners can be trained to provide support for other speakers. This support can involve supplying unknown words,

completing sentences that the speaker has begun, and asking helpful questions to provide language and content support.

3. Repeated tasks can also be a good way of providing support. Initially the speaking may be difficult, but with repetition it can become easier. Techniques like **retelling** can provide this kind of repetition. Another useful technique is **pass and talk**. In this activity each learner has a card with a task on it. The tasks can involve describing something in a picture or in the classroom, saying something about another person on the group, mentioning an item from the current news, or expressing an opinion on something. Each learner in the group has to do the task aloud. After each learner has done their task, the cards are passed around from hand to hand until the teacher says stop. Then each learner must do the task on the card that they are holding. The passing around should happen several times, meaning that the tasks are repeated several times.

4. Informal speaking can be prepared for. As people typically speak about their lives, a good way to prepare for this is to get learners to write a diary describing what they did each day. Every few days the learners get in groups and are asked questions by the others in the group about the content of their diaries.

5. Spoken language uses many more multi-word units than written language. It is worthwhile memorising some of the more useful sentence stems such as, I see, That's right, Are you sure?, Really?, I haven't seen you for ages, What have you been up to? (McCarthy and Carter, 2003).

As most of our speaking tends to be informal speaking, this deserves attention within the classroom.

Formal speaking is affected by all the performance conditions of planning, time pressure, support, and standard of performance described above. We will now look at formal speaking in detail to see how learners can be helped with such speaking. Focusing on formal speaking also provides an excellent opportunity for learners to become aware of what is involved in speaking effectively and can lead to the development of useful planning and delivery strategies.

Formal Speaking

Formal speaking helps language learning in the following ways. It represents a new use of English for most learners and thus requires them to focus on language items that are not as well represented in other uses of the language (Biber, 1989). Formal speaking requires control of content, awareness of a largely passive audience, and being the focus of attention (a rather unsettling experience). It thus requires learners to use language under difficult and demanding circumstances, which will stretch the boundaries of skill development.

In a study of first language speakers of English, Brown, Anderson, Shillcock and Yule (1984) identified the following ways of getting learners to develop their skill in taking a long turn.

1. Learners should experience the task from the listeners' point of view. This enables them to notice things that they should avoid in their own spoken presentation, and helps develop a sense of having an audience.
2. The learners should have the opportunity to work through a series of spoken tasks that gradually increase in complexity. There are several aspects that affect complexity. These include the amount of preparation available, whether the task involves describing a "static" display or "dynamic" process, and the number of items, characters or points to deal with in the information they are presenting. The performance conditions described above also affect the complexity of the task.

The Nature of Formal Speaking

Speaking as a part of work or academic study may involve presenting reports or presenting a viewpoint on a particular topic. This type of speaking has several important features (Brown, 1981).

1. It is transactional. That is, its purpose is to communicate information rather than to maintain social contact as is the case with most interactional speaking.
2. It involves taking a long turn. That is, it is not usually presented as a dialogue but requires speaking for several minutes in a comprehensible and organised way.
3. It is influenced by written language. Often it will involve speaking from notes and will involve academic vocabulary.
4. The speaking is done in the learner's "careful" style in a clear and deliberate way with opportunity for the speaker to monitor the production.
5. It often needs teaching as it is a skill that is not a part of typical language use.

These features have implications for teaching. Let us look at each of them in turn.

Teaching Formal Speaking

The transactional nature of formal speaking means that the effectiveness of the learners' performance should focus on the successful communication of information. Formal speaking opportunities in the classroom should therefore be done with an obvious audience who are interested in the speaker's message. The physical arrangement of the room can affect this. The speaker should face the audience who are sitting in rows or perhaps a horseshoe arrangement. The learners can present **prepared talks** that they give in front of the class or in their group. It is a good idea to have a time limit for the talk, but then to let people ask as many questions as they wish. If the other learners know the subject of the talk they can prepare questions before the talk begins. If the learners are working in small groups, the members of the group can help each other prepare their talks. During each class one or two people can give their talks. The talks may be used as a way of reporting outside reading. Two people may talk on the same subject. One talks in favour of that subject and the other talks against it, somewhat like a small debate (Deyes, 1973). It is best if the learners do not write out their talk and read it, but use short notes to remind themselves of what they want to say. If the class consists of adults in the work force, they can talk about their jobs or some aspects of their experience.

Formal speaking involves taking long turns. Many native speakers find this difficult and so learners need to be aware of the ways of organising a long turn so that it most effectively achieves its goals. This gives a high priority to planning the turn. This planning can be done in several ways.

1. The speaker can look at the ideas that will be presented and find an effective way of organising them. This will usually require a very good knowledge of the content matter of the talk.
2. The speaker can use a standard rhetorical framework for organising the ideas. For example, when presenting a description of something the speaker can present a feature followed by two examples, the next feature and two examples, and so on. If the speaker is defending a viewpoint, the speaker could proceed by systematically eliminating the arguments against that point of view.
3. The speaker can use a standard information framework, such as topic type (see Appendix 2). Thus, when describing how to do something, the speaker describes the materials needed, the tools needed, the steps to go through with cautions and conditions mentioned at some steps, and then the final result, as in the instruction topic type.
4. Group planning activities can be very useful in providing help for a speaker. **Moderation** is an interesting way of doing this. The teacher

writes a topic for discussion on a large sheet of paper. The learners write their ideas about the topic on small pieces of paper. The teacher collects these and puts them in clusters on the large sheet. The learners discuss the ideas to clarify them. If a person disagrees with an idea that person says "Objection!" and that objection is written on a different coloured piece of paper and placed next to the idea. Then the learners think of headings for each cluster. The headings are written on pieces of paper and are added to the large sheet. The next step is for the learners to work on the relative importance of the clusters of ideas. Each learner is given two or three stickers to put on the headings they think are most important. Instead of clusters, a scale or a matrix can be used (Purvis, 1983). This information is then used as the basis for planning a talk.

Formal talks may be scripted. That is, they may be initially in a written form. It is not usually desirable for the talk to consist of simply reading a written paper aloud. Learners thus need to get practice in preparing notes and speaking from brief notes. To encourage this, it may be necessary to use a **pyramid procedure** (Jordan, 1990). This means that the learner works alone to prepare the notes for a talk. Then the learner presents the talk to one learner using the notes, and gets feedback from that learner about the talk. Then using a shorter form of the notes, the learner presents the talk to a small group of three or four learners. Finally, the talk is presented to the whole class using only brief note cards. The practice before the class presentation reduces the need for the notes.

Learners need unthreatening opportunities to speak carefully on topics they know well. They need feedback on what aspects they need to monitor.

Learners need graded tasks, the chance to be listeners in order to get a consumer's view of formal speaking, and a systematic approach to planning and presenting formal talks. These are nicely combined in the **serials** activity. The learners work in groups to prepare a story that will be told part by part over several days. Each group prepares a different story and the other groups respond to each part of the story saying whether it is interesting, well presented, and so on (Hirvela, 1987). The starting point for the story can be a picture (tell the life story of this person), a personal account, a folk tale, a story from a graded reader, or a dramatisation of a newspaper story. Because the learners have the opportunity to be both speakers and listeners, they can develop their understanding of what is involved in making a spoken presentation.

Table 7.1 summarises the main points covered in this section and can act as a checklist for ensuring that a suitable range of activities has been covered to help with formal speaking.

Table 7.1 Features of Formal Speaking and their Implications

Features	Implications for teaching
Transactional	Focus on successful communication to an audience
Long turn	Give a high priority to planning
Written influence	Practise making and using notes
Careful style	Provide well-prepared opportunities to speak carefully
Needs to be taught	Use graded tasks and give learners the chance to be listeners

A Process Approach to Formal Speaking

Because formal speaking is usually a planned activity, it is possible to take a process approach to it. This means dividing the task into parts such as taking account of the goals and the audience, gathering ideas, organising ideas, making a set of speaking notes, and presenting and monitoring the talk (see the companion volume to this book, *Teaching ESL/EFL Reading and Writing*, for a process approach to writing using very similar parts of the process).

An important part of the formal speaking process is taking account of the audience and the suitability of the information that is to be conveyed to them. This involves considering questions such as: Which parts of my information will be the most useful for the audience? Which parts will be difficult for them to understand? What do I want them to gain from my talk? Speakers can gain an awareness of the audience by having experience of being part of the audience, by getting questions and feedback from the audience, and by observing the audience's reactions during a talk. Table 7.2 relates activities and supports to the various parts of the formal speaking process. Taking a process approach is effectively encouraging learners to develop a strategy for dealing with formal speaking. Thus, when a teacher takes this approach learners should be made aware of the parts of the process and how they can take control of them.

It is useful for members of a language class to present tasks to each other so that they experience both the roles of speaker and listener. It is also useful to take part in tasks where there is immediate evidence about whether the speaker understands or not. This can be done with extended **listen and do** type tasks, or with a restatement type of activity like **triads**. In triads A and B have a conversation. C is the referee. One topic for discussion is chosen from a list of fairly controversial topics, such as: "Learners should be paid to go to school", or "Money spent on space travel is a waste". A speaks for a short period of time expressing two or three ideas. B listens carefully then paraphrases what A said. Both A and C, the

Table 7.2 Tasks for Learning the Parts of the Process of Formal Speaking

Parts of the process	Tasks
Goals and audience	Be a listener Talk and get audience feedback Perform **listen and do** tasks where there is an observable outcome of the talk such as something drawn, or made from LEGO
Gathering ideas	**Brainstorm** and **What is it like?** in groups Follow schema such as topic type or discourse plans to gather information systematically
Organising ideas	Use rhetoric plans Discuss and evaluate model outlines Use guiding checklists
Making speaking notes	**Information transfer** Note-taking
Presenting and monitoring	Talk on your speciality **Be an expert** **4/3/2** Prepare, talk to a partner, talk to a group, then talk to the class

referee, listen carefully to B's paraphrase. If B simplifies or changes A's ideas, then either C or A can correct him. If both C and A agree that B's paraphrase is correct, then B may give a few ideas of their own on the discussion topic. A must listen carefully then paraphrase what B said before they can give more opinions of their own. B and C listen and correct A's paraphrase and so on. After five or ten minutes, depending on the teacher, the members of the triad change roles, i.e. B becomes the referee, and A and C discuss, and a new discussion topic is chosen.

A speaker may have difficulty with a talk because there is little to talk about or the topic is poorly understood. A high level of familiarity with the content of a talk is likely to lead to quality in other aspects such as the presentation, formal correctness and awareness of audience. So, good preparation for a talk can involve using group work activities to gather and elaborate the information that will be presented. **Brainstorming** is an effective way of doing this. In this activity learners suggest ideas which are listed uncritically, the main goal being to get as many ideas as possible. Later the ideas are organised and evaluated. An advantage of brainstorming is that it can result in a very diverse collection of ideas. A much more focused way of gathering ideas involves using information schema or self-questioning scales to gather information systematically. Appendix 2 lists one such set of schema (see *Teaching ESL/EFL Reading and Writing* (Nation, 2009) for more on topic types). So, for example, if the talk was about an exciting event, the state/situation topic type could be used. This involves these questions:

Who are the people involved?
When and where did it happen?
What were the background causes?
What happened?
What are the things likely to happen as a result?

Organising ideas clearly relates closely to awareness of the audience and the getting of ideas, and in preparing a talk there could be continual movement between these parts of the process. Is it best to begin the talk with a complete overview, or is it most suitable to begin with an example? Should the talk be divided into quite separate sections? In making such decisions it is useful to look at how others have organised their talks, or rhetorical models such as description by exemplification, or argument by the elimination of alternatives.

Most people speak using written notes as a guide. These probably offer a feeling of security as much as they offer guidance. Learners should practise being able to prepare and present from brief notes. For any particular talk this may mean starting from quite elaborate notes and with practice reducing them. Even very experienced speakers welcome the opportunity to practise their talks with a supportive audience.

The **pyramid procedure** and procedures involving a changing audience like **4/3/2** can provide opportunities for repetition with the speaker using an increasingly reduced form of notes each time. **Information transfer** grids and diagrams are a useful form of notes to guide speaking. Due to their structured nature, they give the speaker a systematic route to follow and allow the audience to predict what will come.

Presenting and monitoring the talk, like all the other parts of the formal speaking process, can be planned for and practised. Repeated opportunity to present is important here. Tactfully designed and used checklists are also useful. Feedback on presentation should lead learners to reconsider other parts of the formal speaking process.

Guidelines for Presenting a Formal Talk

The following guidelines for presenting a formal talk take account of the importance of monitoring the attention of the audience, and communicating a clear message. For a review of research on learning from lectures, see Bligh (1972).

1. The message should be limited to three or four important pieces of information. For example, if the talk is about the speaker's country,

the speaker could limit the main points to three or four features that are most striking about the country. In the case of Singapore, these may be: (1) the importance of its location; (2) its multiracial nature; (3) its strong social policies. These three or four pieces of information should be emphasised by presenting them in a written form as well as a spoken form, by numbering them or signalling them in some other way ("The first important feature is . . ."), and by repeating them in a final summary.

2. The speaker should present or gradually build up a *simple* outline of the main points of the talk. The speaker may wish to present the whole outline at the beginning and work through it. This helps the audience keep up with the talk and allows them to anticipate what comes next.

3. There should be three or four changes of the focus of attention during the talk. This means that the whole talk should not consist of the speaker talking to the audience. The changes of focus of attention provide a rest for the audience, and the speaker, and thus help to keep their attention. Here are some different foci of attention:

   (a) The speaker talks to the audience.
   (b) The audience question the speaker.
   (c) The audience talk to each other in pairs.
   (d) One of the audience talks to the rest of the audience.
   (e) The audience study a handout, see a short film or watch a demonstration.

   If there are too many changes, the audience may lose track of the main message. Here are some examples of the changes in focus of attention used during a complete talk.
   In a talk on the sound system of English:

   (a) The audience listened to the speaker.
   (b) The audience worked on transcribing a few items and reported back to the speaker.
   (c) The audience listened to the speaker again.
   (d) The audience questioned the speaker.

Note in this example that there were two opportunities for the speaker to talk to the audience but there was a change in the focus of attention between these two opportunities so that the second opportunity to talk to the audience was regarded as another change in the focus of attention.

In a talk on his work as a drug enforcement officer:

(a) The audience listened to the speaker.
(b) The audience worked in pairs preparing questions.
(c) The audience questioned the speaker.
(d) The audience listened to the speaker.

Note, in both examples, the sessions began with the audience listening to the speaker. There are two reasons for doing this. At the beginning of the talk the audience is likely to be most attentive and rested, and so this is a good time to get the main points across. Second, the audience are there to listen to the speaker and so the speaker should show that they have interesting and useful information to present and thus establish credibility with the audience.

Note in the second example how the speaker made sure that he would be asked questions, by getting the audience to work in pairs to prepare questions. He introduced the working in pairs by saying this:

> Many people have seen films about the work of drug enforcement officers. The films usually only show the most exciting and often unusual parts of their work. Talk to your neighbour about what you think my work might involve and prepare a question to ask me about it.

4. The audience should be involved in the talk by having a chance to participate through asking questions, providing feedback, and responding to tasks. There are three reasons for this. First, it keeps the attention of the audience. Second, it provides feedback for the speaker about whether the learners are following the talk, where they have difficulty, and what any are interested in. Third, it improves the quality of the information, particularly if some of the audience are already well informed on the topic.

Presenting a formal talk is a worthwhile skill, and it is one that many native speakers have difficulty in learning. It is, however, an important skill and also an important source of language learning opportunities.

Monitoring Formal Talks

The process division of the formal speaking task (shown in Table 7.2) provides a useful basis for monitoring and providing helpful formative feedback. When listening to formal talks both teachers and learners can look analytically to see where the strengths and weaknesses of the speaker lie.

Goals and Audience

- Is the speaker showing awareness of the audience through the use of appropriate language, pace of presentation, and shared experience?
- Is the speaker's goal clear?

Ideas

- Has the speaker enough relevant things to talk about?
- Is the speaker trying to present too much information?

Organisation

- Is the talk well organised?
- Is the organisation of the talk clear to the listeners?

Notes

- Is the speaker talking to the audience?

Presentation

- Is the delivery fluent?
- Does the speaker keep the attention of the listeners?
- Are there enough changes of focus of attention?

Learners should be encouraged to reflect on their own formal speaking, noting what they do well, and where they need to make improvement.

Another kind of long turn is conversational story-telling (Jones, 2001) where, during a conversation, someone tells of an incident that happened to them. Hill and Storey (2003) describe the use of an on-line website to improve oral presentation skills.

Formal speaking pushes learners in their output. It is worth remembering, however, that formal monologue is typically only a small part of most people's speaking.

Speaking with others, as we have seen, can push learners in their output and make them notice gaps in their knowledge. In Chapter 6 on learning through task-based interaction, we saw how negotiation can push learners to change their output and can provide encouragement for speaking skills to develop. Many of the activities described there are very useful for pushing learners' output. Thus, although this chapter has largely focused on formal speaking, this is only one part of a balanced programme in helping learners to learn through speaking.

CHAPTER **8**

Language-focused Learning

Deliberate Teaching

This chapter looks at language-focused learning of vocabulary, grammar, and discourse with the aim of helping learners understand and produce spoken language.

Language-focused learning involves giving attention to features of the language not just for a particular message that they convey, but for their spoken or written form, their general meaning, the patterns that they fit into, or their correct use. For example, the teacher may explain the meaning of a word to learners and show the pattern it fits into, or the learners may work through exercises based on a rule, such as add -*ed* to make the past tense.

Surprisingly, the boundary between language-focused learning and meaning-focused instruction is not so easy to draw. Noticing an item is one of the steps in acquisition. This noticing is arguably attention to language; that is, the temporary decontextualisation of the item so that it is viewed as part of the language system rather than part of the message. In language-focused learning, the attention to the item as part of the system is likely to be teacher directed (through explanation or through the design of an activity), obvious, and not brief. As Fotos and Ellis (1991) show, this attention to language can also be the focus of a communicative activity.

The Value and Limits of Language-focused Learning

There is now considerable evidence to show that language-focused learning can help second language learning. Reviews by Long (1988), Spada

(1997) and Ellis (2006) indicate that language-focused learning can have the following effects.

1. A combination of language-focused learning and meaning-focused use leads to better results than either kind of learning alone.
2. Language-focused learning can speed up the rate of second language acquisition.
3. Language-focused learning may help learners to continue to improve their control of grammar rather than becoming stuck with certain errors.
4. Some language-focused learning can lead directly to acquisition, depending on the kinds of items focused on, especially vocabulary (Elgort, 2007).
5. Language-focused learning can indirectly provide meaning-focused input.

There are, however, limitations on the effect of language-focused learning. These limitations include the following.

1. Language-focused learning cannot change the order in which learners acquire certain complex, developmental features of the language, such as questions, negatives, and relative clauses.
2. Language-focused learning needs to be combined with the opportunity to use the same items in meaning-focused use.
3. Some grammatical items learned through language-focused learning may only be available to the learner in planned use.

The most important finding, however, is that language-focused learning has an important role to play in second language acquisition. The purpose of this chapter is to show what this role is and how it is most effectively played.

Deliberate Vocabulary Learning

The best language-focused vocabulary instruction involves looking at a word as part of a system rather than as part of a message. This means paying attention to regular spelling and sound patterns in words, paying attention to the underlying concept of the senses of words (head of the school, head of a bed, head of a match . . .), paying attention to word building devices, giving attention to the range and types of collocations of a word, and paying attention to the range of clues to the word's meaning provided by context.

It is also useful to study words isolated from context and as individual items. There is substantial research in this area and it shows how learners can take the first steps in quickly learning a large vocabulary (Nation, 2001: 263–316), and that this learning results in implicit as well as explicit knowledge (Elgort, 2007).

Language-focused vocabulary learning has three main values. It speeds up vocabulary learning considerably. It contributes directly to implicit knowledge. It raises awareness of the systematic features of vocabulary. Let us look at each of these.

1. Larsen-Freeman and Long (1993) see one of the clearest findings from research on instructed second language acquisition as being that instruction can speed up the rate of learning. This finding is certainly true for second language vocabulary development. This research has focused on the initial learning of vocabulary and on the quantity of items learned (Nation, 2001: 296–316). There is now a growing body of research on the effect of language-focused learning on the quality of vocabulary knowledge (Webb, 2005; Schmitt and Meara, 1997).

2. Recent research (Elgort, 2007) shows that language-focused vocabulary learning using word cards results in implicit knowledge. That is, as a result of deliberate learning, the vocabulary is subconsciously and fluently available for use, and has entered into lexical relationships with other words. Knowledge of words learned this way is also explicitly available.

3. Just as the grammar of the language contains systematic features, so does the vocabulary. Language-focused attention to these features will speed up the development of explicit knowledge and will also make learners more aware of them when they are met in language use. This awareness will make them more likely to be noticed and thus more likely to be acquired.

The Requirements of Language-focused Vocabulary Instruction

Vocabulary instruction should focus on useful items. We have more frequency information about vocabulary than any other part of the language. What this information shows is that it is essential for learners to have good control over the relatively small number of high frequency words. The most important 2000 to 3000 word families make up such a large proportion of both spoken and written use that it is difficult to use the language effectively without a good knowledge of them. These words can be found in *A General Service List of English Words* (West, 1953) and the Academic Word List (Coxhead, 2000). However, to cope with unsimplified spoken language, a vocabulary size of around 6000 word families is needed (Nation, 2006).

For learners who have a good knowledge of the high frequency words, the focus of instruction should be on learning and coping strategies, including using context clues for inferring meaning, and using word parts and other mnemonic procedures for learning new low frequency words. Learners need to take responsibility for using these strategies to increase their knowledge of low frequency words.

Vocabulary instruction should involve thoughtful processing so that the words are remembered. Teachers should evaluate the procedures they use and the procedures their learners use to see their effectiveness. One way of doing this is to look at them from a "levels of processing" viewpoint (Craik and Tulving, 1975; Baddeley, 1990: 160–173), to see how thoughtful the learners have to be when they use a particular procedure. Evaluating a procedure from this point of view can involve asking questions like these.

- Are the learners giving attention to more than one aspect of the word? For example, meaning, form, use.
- Are the learners being original and creative in the way they look at the word?
- Are the learners relating the word to previous knowledge?

Vocabulary instruction should avoid grouping words that will interfere with each other. Research on the form and meaning relationships between words shows that near synonyms, opposites, free associates, and members of a lexical set such as names of fruit or items of clothing interfere with each other and make learning more difficult if they are learned together (Higa, 1963; Tinkham, 1993, 1997; Waring, 1997; Nation, 2000b). This means that if *fat* and *thin* are both new items for a learner, and if they are learned at the same time, the learner will have difficulty in learning which is which and not mixing them up. Unfortunately most course designers are not aware of this research and deliberately group words in this way.

Vocabulary instruction should take account of the flexibility and creativity involved in normal vocabulary use by drawing attention to the systematic features of vocabulary. This means giving attention to affixes, the underlying meaning of words, and the way they collocate with other words.

Knowledge gained through deliberate learning should be enriched by opportunities to learn through meaning-focused input and meaning-focused output. Language-focused learning is a means to an end and that end is not reached unless learners can easily find the words they need when they are using the language. It is therefore important to make sure that the words that are learned have plenty of opportunity to be used, and to be used fluently.

Techniques and Procedures for Vocabulary Learning

The following description of techniques and procedures has been arranged according to proficiency level—beginner, intermediate, and advanced.

Beginners

There are numerous possibilities for conveying the meaning of new vocabulary (see Nation, 1990, especially Chapter 3; Nation, 2008). Both brief pre-teaching before meeting the words in context (Jenkins, Stein and Wysocki, 1984) and explanation in the context of listening to a story (Ellcy, 1989) have a substantial effect on learning compared to incidental learning without directly focused attention. This means that before listening activities, it is worth drawing learners' attention to some of the vocabulary that will occur and that it is worth learning. This can be done by listing words on the board and quickly discussing them, giving learners lists of words and meanings to work on at home, or by doing a semantic mapping activity drawing on the learners' previous knowledge and introducing the target vocabulary into the map (Stahl and Vancil, 1986).

For adult beginners, it is useful to have a rapid expansion of vocabulary through direct vocabulary learning. An effective way of doing this for older learners is to make use of **vocabulary cards**. These are small cards (about 4cm × 3cm) with the second language word on one side and the first language translation on the other. Particularly at the beginning level, it is useful to have a phrase containing the new word along with the word. Learners use these cards in their own time, looking at them frequently for a short time. It is good to change the order of the cards as they are looked at to avoid a serial effect in learning. The use of such cards should be combined with mnemonic techniques such as the **keyword technique**, or **word part analysis**, or simply creating a mental picture of the word or a situation where it is used. The considerable amount of research on this rote learning procedure clearly shows its effectiveness (Nation, 2001: 296–316; Nation, 2008).

Even at an early stage of language learning, it is worth looking at word building devices. The inflectional suffixes of English are a good start as they are all frequently used.

As the guessing from context strategy is so useful, it is worth practising it as early as possible. At this stage, many of the context clues will come from the situational context rather than the linguistic context. Use of a guided guessing procedure will add some depth of processing to the learning of new words.

At this level, direct teaching of vocabulary is useful. The techniques used can include the use of first language definitions, synonyms, pictures, or demonstration. Some items, particularly numbers, greetings and polite phrases should be practised to a high level of fluency. The teacher can suggest mnemonics for the words, but this should be regarded more as training in getting learners to create their own mnemonics because research indicates that mnemonic tricks created by each learner result in better retention than those provided by others. Here are some examples for learning languages other than English.

- *Nana* (meaning "seven" in Japanese) is easy to learn because the shape of the number 7 is like the shape of a (ba)nana.
- *Khâw* (meaning "rice" in Thai) sounds like *cow* in English. The learner can think of an image of a cow eating rice, or a cow made of rice.
- *Kaiki* (meaning "all of it" in Finnish) sounds a little bit like *cake* in English, so think of an image of someone buying all the cakes in a shop.

Intermediate

An important focus at the intermediate level is expanding the uses that can be made of known words. This means drawing attention to the underlying meaning of a word by seeing its use in a variety of contexts. Exploring the meanings of words like *head*, *fork*, or *agree* can be a useful activity. This type of activity can be done inductively with the learners going in to the underlying meaning through the analysis of many examples, or deductively by going out from a meaning to examples.

The guessing from context strategy should continue to be practised with attention being given mainly to clues in the linguistic context (see Nation, 1990 and 2008, for various ways of doing this).

Word parts should be used to help remember the meanings of new words. These should include affixes from levels 3 and 4 of Bauer and Nation (1993), which include -able, -er, -ish, -less, -ly, -ness, -th, -y, non-, un-, -al, -ation, -ess, -ful, -ism, -ist, -ity, -ize, -ment, -ous, in-, all with restricted uses.

Examples of the **keyword technique** have been given above with *nana*, *khâw* and *kaiki*. It is worth formalising the strategy at this stage. The keyword strategy links the form of an unknown word to its meaning by using a keyword usually taken from the first language. Here is an example. Let us imagine a Spanish-speaking learner of English wants to learn the English word *car*. She then thinks of a Spanish word that sounds like *car*, for example *caro* (which means "expensive"). The learner then has to think of the meanings "car" and "expensive" acting together in an image, for example, a very expensive car. The keyword *caro* thus provides a form and meaning link for the meaning of *car*.

The keyword procedure can be broken into these steps.

1. Look at the second language word and think of a first language word that sounds like it or sounds like its beginning. This first language word is the keyword.
2. Think of the meaning of the second language word and the meaning of the first language word joined together in some way. This is where imagination is needed (Ellis and Beaton, 1993).
3. Make a mental picture of these two meanings joined together.

There are many techniques that can be used at this level to help learning vocabulary.

It's my word! (Mhone, 1988) or **word detectives** involves a learner reporting on a word that was learned out of class recently. The reporting can follow a pattern involving saying where the word was met, what it means, how it is used, and how it can easily be remembered.

Each week the teacher can provide a time for revising the vocabulary worked on previously. One person in the class can be given the job of keeping a note of words to be revised as they occur. During the revision time the words can be dictated in sentences to the learners. They can be put in true/false statements. They can be written on the blackboard for the learners to pronounce or break into parts. They can be used in collocation activities where learners work in groups to put them into a variety of linguistic contexts.

The activities at the beginning and intermediate levels should focus on the essential general service vocabulary of English of approximately 2000 words.

Advanced

At the advanced level, learners who intend to study in English at post-16 level or university need to focus on the academic vocabulary of English. This vocabulary can be found in the 570 word family Academic Word List (Coxhead, 2000). All learners at this level need to refine the strategies they need for dealing with the large number of low frequency words that they will meet. These strategies include, in order of importance, guessing unknown words from context, using word parts to remember the meanings of words, and using mnemonic techniques. At this level, there is little value in the direct teaching of vocabulary although learners should be doing substantial amounts of direct learning using word cards. The main focus of teaching should be on strategy development.

Deliberate Grammar Learning

Grammar can be deliberately learned as a result of direct explanation and analysis, through doing grammar exercises, through consciousness-raising activities, and through feedback. Let us now look at each of these in turn.

Grammar-focused Description

This kind of language-focused learning results in learners being able to say what a grammatical feature means, how it is put together, or how it should be used. As the following techniques show, the instruction is teacher produced description of rules or patterns, learner analysis of examples, or learner manipulation and joining of parts. Direct explanation of grammar points has certain advantages over more communicatively based problem-solving activities (Sheen, 1992). First, the direct teaching gets the point across quickly and allows more time for practice and meaning-focused use. Second, problem-solving group work which focuses on grammar may require vocabulary and constructions that the learners do not know. Discussing grammar is not easy. Sheen conducted a small-scale experiment comparing direct explanation with group problem solving and found that on his written test there was no significant difference, but that there was a significant advantage for direct teaching on his oral test, possibly due to the extra time available for oral practice. Fotos (1993) also found a slight but non-significant advantage for teacher description.

Exploring Collocation Patterns

Some of the simplest explanations that could be of immediate value to learners involve the description of collocation possibilities. Here are some examples, "*dismantle* is usually followed by the name of an elaborate structure, such as *dismantle the organisation, dismantle the machine*; *outdo* is usually followed by the name of a person, *outdo Jones*". Collocation patterns are like "local" rules, and may be of more practical value to a learner than the more generally applied rules (Lewis, 1993).

Learning Explicit Grammatical Rules

In his discussion of consciousness-raising, Sharwood Smith (1981) makes the point that there is a range of knowledge that learners may have. He uses the dimensions of overtness and elaboration to describe these. There are clearly other factors as well, such as generality of application, and kinds of information (rules, strategies, probabilities). There are several exercise types that could fit this category. They include transformation, ordering, constructing from rules, and classification. Let us look at each of these.

Eckman, Bell and Nelson (1988) used **transformation exercises** to teach relative clauses. The learners were given a pair of sentences, such as *I saw a little boy. A woman was carrying him*, to transform into a single sentence. The set of combined sentences made up a story. Before doing the exercise the learners were given a little explanation and teacher-led practice.

In **self-checking pair work**, each learner in a pair has a similar task to do, but the answer to learner A's task is on B's sheet and this is the starting point for B's task. A has the answer to B's task and this answer was the starting point for A's task. Here is an example from Palka (1981).

A	B
I think it may rain.	It looks like it might/may rain
--------------------	--------------------------------
It looks . . .	I think . . .

A has to change their sentence to one beginning with *It looks*. They do this, without telling B their original sentence, and B tells them whether they are right or wrong and corrects them if necessary. B then changes their sentence to one beginning with *I think*, and A tells them if they are correct.

Fotos and Ellis (1991) suggest an integration of meaning-focused and form-focused tasks where the learners have to focus on a message which is about grammar. The task aims to develop explicit knowledge about a grammar point (which may eventually add to implicit knowledge through consciousness-raising or output becoming input), and provides an opportunity for the development of implicit knowledge of other items through the message-focused interaction.

The task that they designed involved groups of four, or pairs. In groups of four, each member had different sentences and they had to decide through group discussion which sentences were correct and which were not. This is a kind of classification activity. All the sentences involved the same grammar point. Finally, the learners had to find the rule to describe the basis for the decision.

Consciousness Raising Activities

Ellis (1991: 232–241) distinguishes practice activities and consciousness-raising activities. Whereas practice activities focus on use through repeated perception or production, **consciousness-raising** activities develop explicit understanding of how a grammatical construction works. The goal of consciousness-raising activities is to help learners notice language items when they appear in meaning-focused input and thus increase the chances that they will be learned. Consciousness-raising activities therefore have limited, delayed aims. They need not result in deliberate production, but develop an awareness of the form, function and meaning of particular items at the level of explicit knowledge. This awareness need not involve the understanding of grammatical terminology. Success in a consciousness-raising activity would be measured by the learner consciously noticing the same item in meaning-focused input and thinking something like "I have seen that before".

Consciousness-raising activities can involve the following.

- having to underline or note examples of an item in a text
- being given examples and having to construct a rule
- having to classify examples into categories such as countable/uncountable or active/passive
- performing rule based error correction
- using a rule to construct a sentence
- recognising instances of a rule in operation.

Language-focused Correction

Tomasello and Herron (1989) suggest that some activities should be designed so that learners make errors and then get immediate feedback to make them aware of the gaps in their knowledge. Their deliberate encouragement of errors through incorrect analogy is called the "garden path" technique. The expression "to lead someone down the garden path" means to deliberately trick someone. It is important to note that it is not the error which is important in the garden path technique, but the noticing which comes from it. Here is a typical garden path activity.

Teacher:	Here is a sentence using these words *think* and *problem. I thought about the problem.* Now you make one using these words *talk* and *problem.*
Learner:	We talked about the problem.
Teacher:	Good. *argue* and *result.*
Learner:	We argued about the result.
Teacher:	Good. *discuss* and *advantages.*
Learner:	We discussed about the advantages.
Teacher:	No. With *discuss* we do not use *about.*

Tomasello and Herron (1989) found that learners who made an error and were immediately corrected learned more than learners who simply had the correct form explained to them. "Students learn best when they produce a hypothesis and receive feedback, because this creates maximal conditions under which they may cognitively compare their own system to that of mature systems. Such comparisons are clearly important in L1 acquisition" (p. 392). Tomasello and Herron argue that because the activity was done as a group rather than an individual activity, there were no negative motivational effects. The learners involved could see that many others were making the same error, and that their errors were deliberately caused by the teacher.

There are two major factors to consider when deciding what to do about errors. The first is the cause of the error and the second is the effect of correction. Error correction as a means of consciousness-raising has several advantages (Ellis, 1990: 193–194). First, it can be a striking way of noticing, particularly if the error interfered with communication of a message. Second, it pushes the learner to notice a gap, exemplified by the difference between the error and the correction. Third, it assists the learning of accurate explicit rules that can be used to produce output that may become input for implicit knowledge.

Ellis (2005 and 2006) describes very useful principles for guiding language-focused grammar learning. These include the following: grammar teaching should focus on form, meaning and use; there should be separate grammar lessons as well as incidental attention to grammar; and corrective feedback is important for learning grammar.

Correcting Grammatical Errors

Correcting errors is best done if there is some understanding of why the error occurred. This involves error analysis. Error analysis is the study of errors to see what processes gave rise to them. Useful surveys of error analysis can be found in Richards (1974), Dušková (1969), and Lennon (1991). Table 8.1 lists some of the causes along with examples.

Table 8.1 Causes and Examples of Second Language Errors

Cause	Example error	Explanation
Interference from the first language	There are too many difference. When I was young I was very sick. But now that I am a virgin I can take care of myself.	The first language does not mark singular and plural. *Virgin* and *adolescent* are the same word in the first language.
Interference from the second language	One factor which aids second language learning to occur.	The use of *aid* is modelled on the use of *help*.
Reduction to increase efficiency	Big square on top of small square.	The learner was under time pressure to complete a task and so left out unnecessary items.
Accidental error	I said . . . told him not to do it.	Self-correction indicates that the learner knows what to say.

Many errors have more than one cause. For example, interference from the first language is encouraged if the learner has to perform beyond their normal level of competence. Then the first language becomes the main resource to fall back on. Errors resulting from the over-use of second language patterns are more likely to occur where the first language patterns provide little support. From a teaching point of view it is thus useful to regard errors as at least partly a result of the conditions under which speaking occurred. Table 8.2 looks at four task-based sources of error, and suggests how a factor in the design of the task could be considered partly responsible for an error the learner makes while doing the task. General solutions are also suggested. The errors the learners make could show first language, second language, efficiency, or accidental influences. It should not be assumed that every error should be corrected or prevented. One of the major contributions of error analysis is the demonstration that some errors are signs of developing competence and will largely disappear when full competence in that particular area is reached.

Table 8.2 shows that teachers can play a part in the control and avoidance of errors. Inevitably, however, errors will occur, and what the teacher then does depends in part on how the teacher regards the effect of correction.

The Effect of Correction

In English we use the phrase "make a mistake". This phrase has two parts, "make" and "a mistake". If a teacher gives most emphasis to "making" or creative language use, then that teacher will have to be prepared to tolerate

Table 8.2 Task-based Sources of Error and Possible Design Solutions

Source of error	Solution
The learners were not sufficiently prepared for the task, or the control of the task was not sufficient.	Check the language, ideas, skill, and text aspects of the task to make sure that at least three of the four aspects are well within the learners' previous experience.
The other learners in the group did not provide support or feedback.	Change the group work activity so that each learner has a particular support job to do and so that the activity has a procedure to make it better organised.
The task was not guided enough; the contribution that the learner had to make was too great.	Redesign the task so that guidance is provided in the area in which the error occurred.
The learner's self-monitoring and coping strategies were not sufficient.	Review the strategies that the learner has for monitoring and checking language production.

mistakes. If a teacher gives most emphasis to "mistakes" and their avoidance, then that teacher will have to reduce the amount of "making" that
the learners do. Reducing the amount of making means getting the learners to take fewer risks in their language use and to do mainly guided
activities. Similarly, continually correcting learners when they make mistakes may have the effect of reducing the amount of "making" that they do.
That is, the continual correction will discourage the learners from speaking
or from saying things that might contain an error.

There is another aspect to the effect of correction. Will the correction be
successful in bringing about a change in the learners' spoken production?
Correcting errors is a part of remedial work.

George (1972) describes the following steps for carrying out remedial
work.

1. The mistakes that the learners make should be found and listed.
2. From that list the teacher should choose a limited number of mistakes or types of mistakes for remedial work. This choice should
   depend on the following points:
   (a) The amount of time that can usually be given for such work.
       Remedial work often takes time that might be used more use-
       fully for teaching new material.
   (b) The possibility of the remedial work being successful. Often, in
       spite of a great deal of effort over a long time, the learners still
       make the same mistakes, like agreement between subject and
       verb, the use of plural forms, etc. If teachers have tried unsuc-
       cessfully for a long time to correct these mistakes, it is unlikely
       that extra remedial work will be successful.
   (c) The feelings of the learners. If the learners are not really worried
       by the mistakes or they see no value in correcting them, remedial
       work will probably be unsuccessful. The learners should be able
       to see that it is possible to make great improvement and that they
       are really learning something useful. Remedial work should not
       be just a reminder of the learners' past failures. Many learners,
       however, welcome remedial work and, particularly where Eng-
       lish is taught as a second language, see English classes as a way of
       getting the informed correction that they do not get outside of
       class.
   (d) The frequency of mistakes. Some mistakes are found very often
       in the learners' speech. Others are rarely found.
   (e) The effect of the mistakes on understanding. Some mistakes are
       found frequently in a learner's work but they do not make it
       difficult for anyone to understand what the learner is trying to

say. Mistakes with a and the, plurals, agreement, and many pronunciation mistakes are like this. Other mistakes, like the use of
stress, vocabulary, and certain sentence patterns, make it very
difficult for someone to understand what the learner is trying
to say. Mistakes like this are not found so often in learners'
work.

(f) The feelings of the listeners or readers about the learners' mistakes. Some mistakes are easily accepted by the speakers of a
certain language while others might make a listener feel that the
speaker who makes the mistake is "uneducated".

3. The teacher should carefully study each mistake chosen, try to find
the reasons why the learners make the mistake, and look at ways for
reteaching or correcting, using new techniques and procedures and a
new way of looking at and explaining the problem. Using new
techniques is very important because there is no value in using
techniques that have already been unsuccessful in dealing with a
particular problem.

4. The teacher should decide whether written activities should be used
to support spoken work.

5. The teacher should see that there is a large number of repeated
opportunities for the learners to give their attention to the features
that the teacher has chosen to correct.

Johnson (1988) suggests that learners need the following four things in
order to get rid of a mistake.

1. The desire or need to get rid of the mistake.
2. An internal representation of what the correct form is like.
3. The ability to know that a mistake has been made.
4. An opportunity to practise the correct form in real conditions.

There are considerable overlaps between George and Johnson's
suggestions.

Correction Procedures

Let us look a little more closely at "new techniques" and the use of written
activities to support spoken work that were mentioned above. If a teacher
decides after careful consideration of the factors mentioned above that
there should be some correction, then it will be more effective if the
teacher uses correction procedures that seem new to the learners. There are
several reasons for this. First, there is little sense in using procedures that
have already been unsuccessful for those learners. They will just remind
them of past failures. Second, a new correction procedure allows the

learner to account for a previous lack of success. "If this way of correcting had been used before, I wouldn't have continued to make the error." Third, a variety of procedures will create more interest in correction.

Here is a list of possible correction procedures with a brief explanation of how each one might work. Hendrickson (1978) provides a well-informed survey of research, theory and practice in error correction.

1. The teacher interrupts and corrects the error, thus providing immediate feedback.
2. The teacher says "What?" each time the error occurs, as if the error made understanding difficult. Research reported by Ellis (1992) indicates that this meaning-focused type of correction is more effective than language-focused correction. This may be because the learners give greater importance to the meaning of messages than their form.
3. The teacher repeats correct forms as if confirming what the learner said. This type of correction is supposed to be like the type of modelling that is done with young native speakers.
4. The teacher makes a written note about the error which is later given to the learners. This type of correction does not interrupt the speaking and may encourage future monitoring.
5. The teacher gives some lesson time to pointing out errors that the learners have made, explains how to correct them, and encourages them to monitor for these errors in future speaking activities. The learners may be reminded to monitor just before the activities. This type of correction relies on awareness and monitoring. Krashen (1981) argues, however, that this monitoring is unlikely to bring about changes in unmonitored language use.
6. The learners practise using correct forms in their "careful" style of speaking. Supporters of a variable competence theory of learning (Ellis, 1986) argue that learning that becomes stable in one style may then be transferred to other less careful styles.
7. The learners practise using techniques like **4/3/2** and **the best recording** which require learners to repeat the same talk several times. Research on this technique (Nation, 1989a) indicates that errors in repeated contexts decrease as a result of repetition. Presumably the repetition reduces the cognitive load and thus allows greater attention to areas of difficulty.
8. The learners do group work that requires accurate performance. This encourages peer correction.

Some researchers and writers on language teaching suggest that teachers should not correct their learners' spoken language. They argue that this affects their creative use of language in that it discourages them from trying new constructions and taking risks. Correction may also make them less receptive to language input because of the embarrassment and other feelings that it may cause. There is, however, a role for correction, particularly if it is directed towards errors that will benefit from attention and if it is done in a way that the learners find acceptable. Teachers need to think through their policy and procedures on correction and should discuss these with their learners. At certain stages in their learning, learners may want correction and may feel that they are missing out if they do not get it.

Holmes and Brown (1976) describe the useful discourse feature that can be turned into a communications strategy (Nation, 1980). Learners can deliberately remember it at as Q-> SA + EI, which means a question (Q) should be followed by a short answer (SA) plus extra information (+EI). This is a strategy that can be used to keep the conversation going.

How long have you been here? (Q)
Three months (SA), and I found it quite difficult at first (+EI)

Alternatively, using Q->SA it is possible to kill a conversation.

Have you been here long? (Q)
Yes. (SA)

Learners can be given training in providing extra information. The extra information can be a feeling, a factual piece of information, or a question. The Q-> SA + EI strategy is a particularly powerful one if used well because it can be used to continue or stop a conversation, to steer a conversation away from an unwanted topic to a wanted or familiar topic, and to take control of a conversation by turning the extra information into a long turn. The strategy is particularly useful in interviews where the person being interviewed can direct the interview by the kind of extra information they provide.

Other useful discourse features that could be given deliberate attention include appeals for help with language, how to take a long turn (see Chapter 7), how to bid for a turn in a conversation, how to be vague and imprecise (Brown, 1979), how to encourage others to continue speaking, and how to turn to different topics.

Stenstrom (1990: 144) has a useful and suggestive list of items which are used in spoken language from the London-Lund corpus.

Apologies:	pardon, sorry, excuse me, I'm sorry, I beg your pardon
Smooth-overs:	don't worry, never mind
Hedges:	kind of, sort of, sort of thing

Expletives:	damn, gosh, hell, fuck off, good heavens, the hell, for goodness sake, good heavens above, bloody hell
Greetings:	hi, hello, good evening, good morning, Happy New Year, how are you, how do you do
Initiators:	anyway, however, now
Negative:	no
Orders:	give over, go on, shut up
Politeness markers:	please
Question tags:	is it, isn't it
Responses:	ah, fine, good, uhuh, OK, quite, really, right, sure, all right, fair enough, I'm sure, I see, that's good, that's it, that's right, that's true, very good
Softeners:	I mean, mind you, you know, you see, as you know, do you see
Thanks:	thanks, thank you
Well:	well
Exemplifiers:	say
Positive:	mhm, yeah, yes, yup

Fitting Language-focused Learning into a Course

Typically too much time has been given to language-focused learning in courses and it has dominated rather than served the learning goals. There are several reasons for this, but the main one probably is that teachers and course designers consider that a language course should systematically cover the important grammatical features of the language. This is a reasonable and praiseworthy principle, as long as it is put into practice in a way that takes into account what we know about second language acquisition and what we learn from corpus linguistics.

1. The limitations placed on language-focused learning by develop-mental structures need to be considered, so that time is not wasted on items that the learners are not ready to learn.
2. Where teaching is directed to structures that the learners are ready to learn, the information must be accurate, simple, and accessible.
3. Teachers and course designers need to be aware that the effect of much language-focused grammar learning will be to add to explicit knowledge, often simply by raising consciousness about items. If this is to contribute to implicit knowledge, further substantial meaning-focused activity is needed.
4. Unfamiliar items tend to be introduced at a rate that is much faster than most learners can manage. This is partly a result of not mak-ing sure that items introduced in language-focused learning also

appear in meaning-focused use and in fluency development activities.

5. Many language items that appear in beginners' courses are not important enough to spend time on. They could be more usefully replaced with items that have a wider range and higher frequency of use (George, 1963; George, 1972; Biber, Johansson, Leech, Conrad and Finegan, 1999).

6. Putting grammatical constructions in contrast when teaching them can make learning more difficult by encouraging interference between the constructions. It is better to focus on one construction and leave contrast for later when the contrasted constructions are being established. For example, contrasting active and passive— "three follows two, two is followed by three"—can result in great confusion.

As a rough rule, language-focused learning should not make up more than about 25 percent of the whole range of contact that learners have with the language. If there is a lot of opportunity for meaning-focused use outside the classroom, then much of the classroom time could be on language-focused learning. If learners' only contact with the language is within the classroom, then less than a quarter of this time should be given to language-focused learning.

The range of language-focused activities could include the following.

1. The study of new items, including sounds, vocabulary, grammatical constructions, pragmatics, discourse. This could involve formal presentation by the teacher, individualised exercises, or group activities. For explicit knowledge, this would have both consciousness-raising and monitored production goals. Some of this study would also add directly to implicit knowledge.

2. Familiarisation and practice of previously met items. This may involve activities such as substitution table practice, and completion, transformation, identification or distinguishing activities. These would have the learning goals of adding to implicit knowledge or monitored production.

3. Formal feedback on performance. This could involve the regular use of feedback activities like dictation, and monitored exercises and talks.

Here are some examples of the language-focused learning in existing programmes.

In a beginners' programme in a country where there was no substantial opportunity to use the language, the class involved regular teaching of vocabulary, set phrases (greetings, politeness formulas) and the explanation of useful patterns. These items were also practised in repetition, pattern practice, and dialogue activities. The course lacked opportunities for feedback and correction. This language-focused learning occupied about 25 percent of the class time.

In a pre-university course in a country where English was the main language outside the classroom, learners were encouraged to use small cards to learn academic vocabulary. There was a regular class time to be tested on these each week, mainly as an encouragement to learning. There was also systematic study of word parts as a means of vocabulary expansion. Learners would do two dictations each week and gave talks on which there was written feedback. These activities occupied about 10 percent of class time.

CHAPTER 9

Developing Fluency

The Nature of Fluency

In this book fluency is used with the same meaning given to it by Schmidt (1992) described below, except that it is not restricted to "the planning and delivery of speech" but is also extended to the comprehension of speech. Fluency has the following characteristics in all of the four skills of listening, speaking, reading and writing.

1. Fluent language use involves "the processing of language in real time" (Schmidt, 1992: 358). That is, learners demonstrate fluency when they take part in meaning-focused activity and do it with speed and ease without holding up the flow of talk. There are observable signs that can be used to measure changes in fluency (Arevart and Nation, 1991; Lennon, 1990). These include speech rate (as measured in words or syllables per minute) (Griffiths, 1991a and b), number of filled pauses such as <u>um</u>, <u>ah</u>, <u>er</u>, and number of unfilled pauses.

2. Fluent language use does not require a great deal of attention and effort from the learner.

3. If we consider the four goals of Language, Ideas, Skill, Text (LIST), fluency is a skill. Although it depends on quality of knowledge of the language, and its development involves the addition to and restructuring of knowledge, in essence it involves making the best possible use of what is already known.

These three characteristics of fluency—message-focused activity, easy tasks, and performance at a high level—are also the main characteristics of activities designed to develop fluency.

Fluency and Accuracy

Usually a distinction is made between fluency and accuracy and between activities that are designed to develop fluency and accuracy. This distinction is difficult to maintain. Nation (1989a) and Arevart and Nation (1991) found that an activity that was designed to bring about an increase in fluency, also resulted in a reduction of errors and an increase in grammatical complexity. As the ease increases with which learners make use of what they know, then they are able to give more attention to the quality of what they use.

Thus, a very useful further distinction can be made between fluency, accuracy and complexity (Skehan, 1998). Fluency is typically measured by speed of access or production and by the number of hesitations; accuracy by the amount of error; and complexity by the presence of more complicated constructions, such as subordinate clauses.

Schmidt's (1992) comprehensive review of the psychological mechanisms underlying second language fluency shows that it is not possible to account for developments in fluency simply through an increase in speed of processing. Substantial increases in fluency also involve changes in the nature of the knowledge of language. Anderson's (1989) ACT* theory of skill development includes joining sequences into larger units, broadening the use of some rules, narrowing the scope of others, and strengthening those that are most effective. Cheng (1985: 367) sees restructuring as the essential feature underlying skilled performance. Restructuring involves changing the integration and organisation of knowledge components so that "the procedure involving the old components [is] replaced by a more effective procedure involving the new components". Even theories that see repeated practice as the major determinant of development see fluency as being related to a change in knowledge. It is therefore not surprising that developments in fluency are related to developments in accuracy.

Developing Fluency

Fluency is likely to develop if the following conditions are met.

1. *The activity is meaning-focused.* The learners' interest is on the communication of a message and is subject to the "real time" pressures and demands of normal meaning-focused communication (Brumfit, 1984: 56–57).
2. *The learners take part in activities where all the language items are*

within their previous experience. This means that the learners work with largely familiar topics and types of discourse making use of known vocabulary and structures. These kinds of activities are called "experience" tasks because the knowledge required to do the activity is already well within learners' experience.

3. *There is support and encouragement for the learner to perform at a higher than normal level.* This means that in an activity with a fluency development goal, learners should be speaking and comprehending faster, hesitating less, and using larger planned chunks than they do in their normal use of language. A fluency development activity provides some deliberate push to the higher level of performance often by using time pressure.

There needs to be substantial opportunities for both receptive and productive language use where the goal is fluency. There must be plenty of sustained opportunity either inside or outside the classroom to take part in meaning-focused experience tasks. If the items that have been learned are not readily available for fluent use, then the learning has been for little purpose.

Designing Fluency Activities

How can we design fluency activities that make use of the three conditions mentioned above? Fluency activities depend on several design requirements and features to achieve their goal. These can appear in a variety of techniques over the whole range of language skills. By looking at these requirements and features we can judge whether an activity will develop fluency in an efficient way and we can devise other activities that will. Let us look first at a well-researched activity. The **4/3/2** technique was devised by Maurice (1983). In this technique, learners work in pairs with one acting as the speaker and the other as listener. The speaker talks for four minutes on a topic while their partner listens. Then the pairs change with each speaker giving the same information to a new partner in three minutes, followed by a further change and a two-minute talk.

From the point of view of fluency, this activity has these important features. First, the user is encouraged to process a large quantity of language. In 4/3/2 this is done by allowing the speaker to perform without interruption and by having the speaker make three deliveries of the talk. Second, the demands of the activity are limited to a much smaller set than would occur in most uncontrolled learning activities. This can be achieved through the teacher's control, as is the case in most receptive fluency activities such as reading graded readers or listening to stories, or it can be done by choice, planning or repetition on the part of the learner. In the

4/3/2 activity the speaker chooses the ideas and language items, and plans the way of organising the talk. The 4- and 3-minute deliveries allow the speaker to bring these aspects well under control, so that fluency can become the learning goal of the activity. Note that the repetition of the talk is still with the learner's attention focused on the message because of the changing audience. Third, the learner is helped to reach a high level of performance by having the opportunity to repeat and by the challenge of decreasing time to convey the same message.

Easy Tasks

Experience tasks for the development of fluency involve making sure that the language, ideas and discourse requirements of the activity are all within the learners' experience so that the learners are able to develop the skill aspect (in this case, fluency) of the activity. In listening tasks this is usually done through teacher control, with the teacher controlling the language by working from a simplified text or by consciously controlling the level of the input. However, it can also be achieved by using learner control. This is done for listening activities by getting learners to provide input for other learners, such as when learners present short talks to the class. In speaking activities, allowing learners to provide their own topics and to speak based on their own writing, for example, provides learner control which makes the activity an experience task and thus suitable for the development of fluency.

Message Focus

Having a clear outcome to an activity encourages a meaning focus because the learners use language to achieve the outcome. Commonly used outcomes in spoken activities include completion; distinguishing, matching, classifying; ranking, ordering, choosing; problem solving; listing implications, causes, and uses; data gathering; and providing directions. Some activities, like 4/3/2, do not have a demonstrable outcome but are meaning-focused because the speaker has a strong sense of speaking to an audience, even though it may only be an audience of one person.

Time Pressure

One way of encouraging learners to reach a higher than usual level of performance is by limiting the time in which they can do something. This is used in 4/3/2 by decreasing the time for each repetition. In split information activities like **same or different** or **find the difference**, it is done by putting a time limit on each set of five items and getting learners to change partners after the set time.

Learners may also keep a regular record of how long it takes them to perform a task, and then try to reduce the time it takes them. This could be done with learners recording a description of an object or reading aloud.

Planning and Preparation

Another way of reaching a higher than usual level of performance is to work on the quality of the performance. This can be done through having an opportunity for planning and preparation. Crookes (1989) investigated learners who were given ten minutes to plan what words, phrases and ideas that they would use in their explanation of how to build a LEGO model or complete a map. He found that, compared to learners who were not given time to plan, the learners who planned produced longer utterances, and produced more grammatically complex speech.

Planning and preparation can be done individually, with the help of guide sheets, or in groups. Before doing a same or different split information activity, all the learners who are A get together and work on what they will say. Similarly all the learners who are B get together and plan and practice. After this has been done the As pair up with the Bs to do the activity.

There are numerous ways of designing a planning and preparation element into listening and speaking activities. Here are some brief suggestions of things to do before the fluency activity begins.

- brainstorming the topic
- pre-reading on the topic
- observation of others doing the activity
- repeated opportunities to do the activity
- preparing and practising in the first language
- prediction activities.

The purpose of the preparation is to make the quality of the subsequent listening or speaking reach a higher level than it would without the preparation.

Repetition

Repetition of an activity is a sure way of developing fluency with the particular items and sequences used in the activity. It is necessary to change the audience when designing repetition into meaning-focused speaking activities so that the speaker does not change the spoken message to try to retain the interest of an audience that has already heard the message. The success of repetition activities largely depends on the repetitions involving substantially the same message. In the 4/3/2 activity, the work is done in pairs and the listener in each pair is replaced by a different listener for each repetition.

In listening activities, the purpose for listening may need to change in order to keep the learner interested in the repeated message.

Fitting Fluency into a Course

Many of the techniques described in Chapter 3 on learning language through listening, such as **listen and draw**, and **information transfer**, are easily adapted to meet the conditions for developing fluency. It is likely that the two goals of learning new language items and the development of fluency can be reached in the same activities, provided the conditions for both kinds of learning occur.

Where the second language is not used outside the classroom, it is very important that about a quarter of class time is given to fluency activities.

Only a relatively small amount of knowledge is needed for successful language use. It is important that this knowledge is available for use and therefore a part of class time should be given to fluency activities. Brumfit (1985) suggests: "Right from the beginning of the course, about a third of the total time could be spent on this sort of fluency activity, and the proportion will inevitably increase as time goes on."

If fluency activities are included in each lesson and make use of new language items taught in that lesson, then these items should occur at a low density in the fluency material. In listening material this means that at least 99 percent of the running words should be very familiar to the learners. A second alternative is to include fluency activities in each lesson that make use of items learned several days or weeks before. A third alternative is periodically to give large blocks of time to fluency activities. This suggestion corresponds to Brumfit's (1985) "syllabus with holes in it". These holes or gaps are times when no new material is presented and there are fluency directed activities.

Many fluency techniques involve the linking of skills. For example, reading is followed by listening, discussion is followed by listening, writing is followed by speaking. The reason for linking skills in this way is so that the earlier activities can provide preparation and support for the later activity. This preparation and support then allows a high level of performance to be reached in the later activity—much higher than there would have been if the later activity had not been linked with earlier activities.

If fluency is the goal of a unit of work, it is useful to look at the unit to check the following points.

1. Do the early parts of the unit usefully prepare for the later parts? One way to find the answer to this question is to regard the final part of the unit as an experience task. As fluency is a skill goal, the earlier

parts of the unit should bring the language, ideas, and text features within the experience of the learners.

2. Does the final part of the unit represent the fluency learning goal of the unit?

There are other justifications for linked skill units besides the fluency goal. These include: (1) the need to learn prerequisite items or skills before doing a task; (2) the wish to practise some aspect of language or language use intensively; (3) the cultural logic of the linked activities (i.e., the activities are usually linked in the world outside the classroom, such as read a letter, discuss the contents, write a reply); (4) the need to get learners to repeat vocabulary and grammatical items to help learning; and (5) practicality (it is easier for the teacher to make material that follows on from previous work. It is also easier for the learners to understand). When making a linked skills unit it is worth considering what the justifications for the linking are. This then allows the teacher to see if the linking is being done in the most effective way.

Developing Fluency in Listening and Speaking

Although fluency activities are aimed at the development of a skill, they inevitably affect knowledge of the language. The way that they affect this knowledge in turn relates to the development of fluency. We can distinguish three approaches to fluency development which can all usefully be part of a language course.

The first approach relies primarily on repetition and could be called "the well-beaten path approach" to fluency. This involves gaining repeated practice on the same material so that it can be performed fluently. The second approach to fluency relies on making many connections and associations with a known item. Rather than following one well-beaten path, the learner can choose from many paths. This could be called "the richness approach" to fluency. This involves using the known item in a wide variety of contexts and situations. Most of the suggested techniques in this chapter follow this approach. The third approach to fluency is the aim and result of the previous two approaches. This could be called "the well-ordered system approach". Fluency occurs because the learner is in control of the system of the language and can use a variety of efficient, well-connected, and well-practised paths to the wanted item.

Techniques for Developing Fluency in Listening

All the techniques described here set up the following conditions that are necessary for the development of fluency.

1. The techniques involve meaning-focused activity. They involve listening to interesting stories, puzzle and quiz activities, and activities with clear communication outcomes.
2. They place very limited demands on the learners in that they rely heavily on language items, topics and experiences with which the learners are already familiar. This familiarity may come from having met or produced the material themselves in a different medium, or through drawing on knowledge gained through the first language. The demands of the task may also be limited through the use of controlled input and through the use of supporting material, such as the use of pictures and written texts to support the listening input.
3. The techniques encourage learners to reach a high level of performance through the use of meaning-focused repetition, increasing speed of input, and the opportunity for prediction and the use of previous background knowledge.

In listening and reading activities, a distinction is sometimes made between activities where the learner brings a lot of topic-related background knowledge to the task (top-down processing) and activities where the learner relies primarily on the language of the text to understand (bottom-up processing) (Richards, 1990). Most comprehension activities are a combination of these two approaches, but usually one is predominant. Fluency tasks should be largely top-down processing because these are the ones that allow learners to perform at speed without having to puzzle over language forms.

Top-down processing is encouraged by getting learners to listen when the topic is very familiar to them, when the organisation and other genre conventions are familiar to them, when their attention is strongly focused on the message, and when there is not a concern for linguistic detail.

Bottom-up processing occurs when the main source of information is the text itself and the listener cannot draw on preparation and previous experience to assist in comprehension. Top-down and bottom-up processing tasks usually have different learning goals and set up conditions for different kinds of learning.

The following techniques are roughly graded from those most suitable for beginners to those most suitable for advanced learners.

In the **name it!** activity, the teacher says some sentences that describe something, for example:

"We use it to clean our teeth."

The learners answer by saying or writing the name of the thing that is described, or by choosing it from a group of pictures, or by choosing its name from a group of words on the blackboard. The learners can have a list of multiple-choice answers in front of them. They listen to the sentence and then choose the answer. The items that are described are all things that the learners are familiar with through everyday experience.

Listening to questions is an activity where the teacher asks the learners questions and they answer them. The questions can be based on a picture, a reading passage, or general knowledge. When asking questions the teacher should ask the question before pointing to a learner to answer it. In this way everyone in the class tries to think of the answer in case the teacher points to them. As well as questions, true/false sentences can be used. Each sentence has a number. The teacher says

"Number one: A bicycle has three wheels."

The learners write 1F. The teacher says

"Number two. I am a teacher."

The learners write 2T. (F means False, T means True.)

Questions can easily become a game, with different teams trying to beat the others.

A variation of this technique is to put the answer to each question, either a single word, a short phrase, or a sentence, in a list on the blackboard, but the answers are in a different order from the teacher's questions. The learners must listen to the teacher's question, choose the correct answer, and write it. So, for example, the teacher says:

"What colour is my handkerchief?"

The learners look at this list which is on the blackboard, and choose the answer.

at home   white   a book   paper   at six o'clock

Blown-up books are a useful way of using listening to introduce learners to reading and getting them excited about reading. These very large books have pages which are about eight times the size of ordinary pages and they contain plenty of pictures. As they are so large they can be shown to the whole class while the teacher reads them aloud and all the learners can see the words and pictures. These books can be bought or they can be made by using a photocopier that enlarges what it copies (see Nation, 2009 *Teaching ESL/EFL Reading and Writing* for more information on blown-up books).

The teacher reads the story to the learners while they look at the words and pictures. The same story will be read several times over several weeks and the learners will soon be able to say parts of the sentences that they recall from previous readings. This technique is also useful for listening fluency as the teacher can read the story a little faster each time.

A **listening corner** is a place where the learners can listen to tapes as part of self-access activities. The teacher makes a tape of a spoken version of writing that the learners have already done. The writing could be done individually or as group compositions. Instead of learner compositions learners can listen to recordings of what they have read before (in English or the first language), such as the reading texts from earlier sections of the coursebook.

The **listening to pictures** technique (McComish, 1982) is a way of providing quantity of input. Because of the support that the pictures provide and because of the opportunities for repetition using the same picture, this is also a useful fluency technique.

Listening to stories is particularly suitable for learners who read well but whose listening skills are poor. The teacher chooses an interesting story, possibly a graded reader, and reads aloud a chapter each day to the learners. The learners just listen to the story and enjoy it. While reading the story the teacher sits next to the blackboard and writes any words that the learners might not recognise in their spoken form. Any words the learners have not met before may also be written, but the story should be chosen so that there are very few of these. During the reading of the first chapters the teacher may go fairly slowly and repeat some sentences. As the learners become more familiar with the story, the speed increases and the repetitions decrease. Learner interest in this activity is very high and the daily story is usually looked forward to with the same excitement people have in television serials. If the pauses are a little bit longer than usual in telling the story, this allows learners to consider what has just been heard and to anticipate what may come next. It allows learners to listen to language at normal speed without becoming lost. See the Extensive Reading Foundation website for good books.

In **listen again** the teacher retells a story that the learners have already heard before, but uses different words from the previous telling. The learners are told that one of the events in the story will be different from the previous telling. They listen and note the difference.

In a **visit and listen** activity, the teacher and the learners visit a place outside the school such as a zoo, a factory, a special school, or a fire station. They take notes during the visit and when they return to the school, the teacher talks to them about the visit. This is a kind of linked skills activity.

Listening while reading involves the learners listening to a text and looking at a copy of the text while they listen. Before listening to the passage, the learners can have time to read it or read something containing much the same ideas or vocabulary.

Listening in a controlled vocabulary can be done using **peer talks**. Learners prepare talks to deliver to the whole class or to a small group. These talks help improve listening skills because the level of the language used is usually well suited to the listeners. For adult learners the topics can focus on the speaker's job or special skills. For younger learners the topics may be based on an article in the newspaper, an interesting event, or a story that the learner has just read. Farid (1978) suggests allowing learners to question the speaker after the talk and then to question each other on their understanding of the talk.

Recorded **interviews** can be an interesting source of listening material. Simpson (1981) suggests getting non-native speakers to interview native speakers. This has two good effects. First, it puts the non-native speaker in control of the type of questions to ask and the amount of information given and, second, it makes the interviews more accessible for non-native listeners because the person being interviewed is speaking to a non-native speaker. The non-native speaker interviewer can also include lots of clarification requests and understanding checks which will help the listeners. While listening, the learners can fill in an information transfer chart or complete statements.

In a **predicting** activity the learners are given some information about a talk and have to predict what will occur in the talk. After they have made their predictions, they listen to the talk and see if their predictions were correct. The information that they are given can include a set of incomplete statements, a table of statistics, the title of the talk, or the introductory section of the talk (Watts, 1986). This is a kind of linked skills activity because discussion (the predicting) is followed by listening.

Techniques for Developing Fluency in Speaking

The following speaking fluency activities make use of repetition and rehearsal and are discreet activities. It is also possible for theme-based work over several days to develop into fluency development opportunities.

The **4/3/2** technique has already been described. It combines the features of focus on the message, quantity of production (the speakers speak for a total of nine minutes), learner control over the topic and language used, repetition, and time pressure to reach a high rate of production through the decreasing amount of time available for each delivery.

The best recording is a useful fluency activity involving a tape or digital recorder or the language laboratory. The learner speaks onto the tape talking about a previous experience or describing a picture or set of pictures. The learner listens to the recording noting any points where improvement could be made. Then the learner re-records the talk. This continues until the learner is happy with the recording. This technique can involve planning and encourages repetition through the setting of a quality-based goal.

The **ask and answer** technique (Simcock, 1993) is a follow-up to reading. The learners read a text to a high level of comprehension and then they work in pairs with one learner questioning the other about the text from a list of teacher-prepared questions. The answers to these questions provide a summary of the ideas in the text. The goal of the activity is for learners to perform the asking and answering in front of the class at a high level of fluency, so each pair practises asking and answering several times before doing their class presentation.

Rehearsed talks involve learners using the pyramid procedure of preparing a talk individually, rehearsing it with a partner, practising it in a small group, and then presenting it to the whole class.

Activities described in other chapters of this book can be used to develop spoken fluency if the three conditions of limited demands, meaning focus, and a high level of performance are met. These activities include **ranking**, **information transfer**, **split information** activities, and **interviews**. Repeating an activity that was previously done with a language learning goal is a useful way of developing fluency. A gap of about a week or two is probably sufficient for enough memory of the previous activity to remain.

Monitoring Fluency Tasks

Examining the Context of the Material

When using experience tasks for language teaching, it is useful to have a way of checking to see what parts of the task are within the learners' experience and what part of the task is being focused on as the learning goal. In Chapter 1 we looked at four sets of goals—Language item goals; Idea or content goals; Skill goals; and Text or discourse goals. The mnemonic LIST can be used to remember these goals. A useful rule to follow is that any experience task should have only one of these goals and the other three should already be within the learners' experience. So, if the teacher wants the learners to master the ideas or content of a text, then the language items (vocabulary, grammar, language functions) should all be within the learners' experience.

So, when checking an experience task, it is useful to ask these two questions.

1. What is the learning goal of the task?

2. Are the three other aspects of the task kept within the learners' experience?

Examining the Teaching Material

The following checklists can be used to look at material and activities to develop fluency. They focus on the conditions needed for fluency development.

Table 9.1 Fluency Checklists

A checklist for examining fluency material

1 What will keep the learners interested in the message involved in the activity?
2 How is the activity made easy for the learners to do?
3 What encouragement is there for the learners to perform at a faster than usual level?

A checklist for observing a listening fluency activity

1 Are the learners interested in the message?
2 Are the learners easily able to understand the message?
3 Is the message coming to the learners at a rate that stretches the fluency of the learners?

A checklist for observing a speaking fluency activity

1 Are the learners interested in the activity and its outcome?
2 Are they easily able to find things to talk about?
3 Are they speaking without a lot of hesitation?
4 Are they speaking at a fast rate?

Fluency activities can also be monitored to see if learners are increasing the fluency with which they deal with tasks. Lennon (1990) found that over a period of several months, the measures that showed a change were speech rate and filled pauses. It would be necessary to make careful transcripts of recorded spoken production to measure such change, but teachers may be able to make more subjective judgements that are of value.

Fluency is often a neglected strand of a course, probably because the teacher feels that new material needs to appear in each lesson. Fluency development activities are a very useful bridge between knowing and using.

CHAPTER **10**

Monitoring and Testing Progress

Monitoring Progress

Careful observation of learners while they are involved in listening and speaking activities can provide useful information of their progress. However, if a teacher sets up an information gathering system, then more useful and reliable information can be obtained. Here are some suggestions for doing this.

1. Where possible, get learners to keep a record of their performance on regular classroom activities. For example, learners could record their dictation scores on their own graphs. To do this the number of errors per 100 words of dictation would have to be calculated, but this is not difficult if the length of each dictation passage is known. Similarly, learners could also record their scores on 50-item split information activities (see Figures 10.1 and 10.2).

2. The teacher uses simple observation checklists when learners are performing listening and speaking activities. Many of them have been described in this book.

3. The teacher gets learners to do regular self-assessment of their progress as well as gathering evaluative feedback from them regarding the course. There are good reasons for getting the learners involved in making self-assessment criteria regarding their participation in speaking activities.

4. The teacher crosses items off a syllabus list when satisfied that the learners are able to cope with that part of the syllabus. Appendix 3

was adapted from van Ek and Alexander (1980) to be the basis of a home tutoring course for beginners. Appendix 1 is for a very short course in survival language.

5. The learners build up a sequenced portfolio of completed activities and feedback, where this is possible. This can show improvement during the course.
6. The teacher does regular testing.

Testing Listening and Speaking

Like any tests, satisfactory tests of listening and speaking have to fulfil three criteria—reliability, validity, and practicality. Usually some compromise has to be made between the criteria because what is most reliable might not be the most valid, and what is the most valid might not be practical.

Reliability

A reliable test is one whose results are not greatly affected by a change in the conditions under which it is given and marked. For example, if a test is given on different days by different people it should still give the same results. If the same answer paper is marked by different people, the score should be the same.

There are ways of checking statistically to see if a test is reliable. They all share similar features, but they look at different aspects of reliability. One way of checking is called test/retest. In this procedure the same test is given to the same people twice, usually with a gap of a week or so between the first test and the retest. A reliable test should give very similar results on the two occasions. Another way of checking is called split halves. In this procedure the test is given to a group of learners and then when the test is being marked the items in the test are split into two groups. For example, if the test had 50 items, all the odd numbered items would be put into one group, and all the even numbered items would be in the other. The scores for the two groups of items are compared. For a reliable test the scores for the two groups of items would be similar. A third way of checking is to make two equivalent forms of the same test. The two forms should be as similar to each other as possible without being exactly the same. When the same learners are tested with the two forms of the test, the scores for the two forms should be similar. What is common about all of these ways of checking reliability is that they are trying to see if the test does the same job on all occasions that it is used. If performance on the test keeps changing when the same learners sit it again, it cannot be measuring what it is supposed to be measuring. A reliable test is not necessarily a valid test, but an unreliable test cannot be valid.

There are several features of listening and speaking tests that affect their reliability and teachers can use these to guide their making and use of tests.

1. A listening test will be more reliable if the material that the learners listen to is on tape. The tape recording ensures that whenever the test is used, the speed of speaking and the accent will be the same. This assumes that the quality of the tape-recorder playing the tape and the room in which the tape is played provide consistent conditions. Note that tape-recording the listening input could make the test less valid.
2. A test is more reliable if it has several points of assessment. This means, for example, that a listening test consisting of 50 separate multiple-choice or true-false items is likely to be more reliable than a test involving 12 questions based on a listening text. A test of speaking is more reliable if the speaker is assessed on several speaking tasks and on several sub-skills of speaking rather than on one.
3. A test is more reliable if it can be marked in relation to a set of correct answers or if the marking is based on clearly understood criteria. Sometimes it is worth giving markers some training if several are involved. Marking a dictation or scoring a role play, for example, requires a good understanding of the marking criteria plus some marking practice and discussion. Sometimes it is necessary to have two markers for scoring interviews or role plays (as well as making a recording for later reassessment if the two markers significantly disagree).
4. A test will be more reliable if the learners are all familiar with the format of the test. It is worth giving a little practice in answering a particular type of test before it is used for testing.

Validity

A test is valid if it measures what it is supposed to measure and when it is used for the purpose for which it is designed. This last part of the definition of validity is important because a test may be valid when it is used for a particular purpose but not valid when it is used for another purpose. For example, a pronunciation test may be valid as a test of pronunciation but not valid as a test of spoken communicative ability. For a very clear discussion of authenticity and validity, see Leung and Lewkowicz (2006).

There are several kinds of validity, but because we are concerned with measuring progress and diagnosis, the two kinds that most concern us are face validity and content validity (Davies, 1990: 24).

Face validity is a very informal judgement. It simply means that the people sitting the test, the people giving the test, and others affected by it such as parents, employers, and government officials see the test as fair and reliable. A reliable test which may have good content and predictive validity may be so different from what the public expect or consider relevant that its poor face validity is enough to stop it being used. Good face validity is not a guarantee of reliability or other kinds of validity.

Content validity involves considering whether the content of the test reflects the content of the skill, language, or course being tested. For example, in order to decide if a test of academic listening skill has content validity, we would need to decide what are the components of the academic listening skill and how is this skill used. We might decide that academic listening involves note-taking, dealing with academic vocabulary, and seeing the organisation of the formal spoken discourse. Typically the listener has had some opportunity to read on the topic or it is one of a series of related lectures. Lectures are typically delivered at a certain speed (data on speech rates can be found in Tauroza and Allison (1990)). The next step is to see how well the test includes these components and to see if it includes components that are not part of normal academic listening. If the content of the test matches well with the content of the skill, the test has high content validity. If the test does not cover the components of the skill well, or includes other components that are not part of the skill, or requires the learner to process the components in an unusual way, then it has low content validity. For another example, it is interesting to consider the content validity of dictation as a test of listening skill. What components of listening are not included in dictation? What are the components of dictation which are not typically part of the listening skill? Is the process of listening to a dictation like ordinary listening?

Kellerman (1990) stresses the importance of being able to see the speaker while listening, especially under conditions of difficulty as in listening to a foreign language. Video can thus add an aspect of validity to a test that audiotape does not.

Practicality

Tests have to be used in the real world where there are limitations of time, money, facilities and equipment, and willing helpers. There is no point in designing a one hundred item listening test that is too long to fit into the 40 minutes which are available for testing. Similarly, a speaking test which requires two or more testers to spend 20 minutes with every learner individually will be very expensive to run and will not be practicable if there is not money available.

Practicality can be looked at from several aspects: (1) economy of time, money, and labour; (2) ease of administration and scoring; and (3) ease of interpretation. Practicality can only be accurately determined in relation to a given situation, but generally a practical test is short (notice that this may conflict with reliability), does not require lots of paper and equipment, does not require many people to administer it, is easy to understand, is easy to mark, has scores or results which are easy to interpret, and can be used over and over again without upsetting its validity. It is not easy to meet all these requirements and still have a reliable and valid test. Most tests are a compromise between the various criteria. When making the compromise it is important that validity is not lost.

In a well-reported large-scale project, Walker (1990) demonstrated how it is possible with limited resources to test the speaking proficiency of enormous numbers of learners. Learners had sat a written test in previous years but now the written test was to be replaced with a spoken test to encourage more focus on speaking in the course leading up to it. So, all the learners were tested by an individual interview on a graded reader they had read (about five minutes) and by general conversation on a topic like Holidays, Accommodation, or Language Study (two minutes), totalling seven minutes. The time available to each learner was calculated by estimating the total staff time used for the old written test, and then allocating the same time to the oral test. In the case of Walker's language department, this turned out to be two full working days for the entire teaching staff of 30. This ensured that in terms of time and staff effort, the oral testing of around 1000 learners was practical. Reliability was controlled by (1) using an interview format that was the same for everybody with clearly described types of information to cover and well explained criteria on a five-point scale for judging; (2) systematically training all the testers; (3) monitoring the testers during the testing; and (4) checking statistically that all the testers were consistent in relation to each other in assigning grades.

The Effect of a Test on Teaching

One further criterion for a test is the influence of the form and the content of the test on the classroom (this is sometimes called the "washback" effect). For example, many schools do not test learners' oral proficiency in English. As a result much classroom time is spent on the skills like reading and listening that are tested and very little time is spent on practising speaking because it is not in the test. Here is another example. If the listening test is made up of true/false statements, this could have the effect of very little work being done on listening beyond the sentence level. A good test sets a good model for what should happen in the classroom.

Listening Tests

This section and the following one contain descriptions of a wide variety of listening and speaking test procedures. While looking at the test procedures, it is worth considering the reliability, validity, and practicality criteria that have been looked at above.

Dictation

The teacher reads aloud a text of approximately 150 words phrase by phrase. The learners write each phrase as they hear it. This kind of test has been used as a test of general language proficiency (Oller, 1979).

Partial Dictation

The learners have an incomplete written text in front of them. As they listen to a spoken version of the text, they fill in the missing parts on the written text.

Text with Questions

The learners have a list of multiple-choice questions in front of them while they listen to a text being read or a recorded dialogue. As they listen they answer the questions.

Responding to Statements

The learners listen to statements or questions and respond to them by choosing from multiple-choice items of words or pictures, by indicating true or false, or by giving a short answer.

Three Choice True-false

Instead of responding to statements with just true or false, three categories of response are allowed true, false, opinion (Emery, 1980), or true, false, not stated.

Recorded Cloze

The learners listen to a tape recording where every 15th word has been replaced by a "bleep" sound and with pauses at the end of each sentence. As they listen the learners write the missing words (Templeton, 1977).

Information Transfer

The learners listen to a description or dialogue and label a diagram or fill in a chart or table while they listen. Palmer (1982) describes a wide range of possibilities for information transfer.

Rating Scales and Lists

Based on learners' performance on a task or based on teachers' knowledge of their learners, teachers indicate on a scale where they consider their learners are in terms of listening proficiency. The Australian Second Language Proficiency Ratings, for example, use a nine-point scale ranging from zero proficiency to native-like proficiency. The third point on the scale, *elementary proficiency*, is described as "Able to comprehend readily only utterances which are thoroughly familiar or are predictable within the areas of immediate survival needs". The sixth point on the listening scale, *minimum social proficiency*, is described as "Able to understand in routine social situations and limited work situations" (Ingram, 1981 and 1984). Rating scales may also be used for self-assessment. Learners look at the items in a list, preferably of functions such as "I can use the telephone", "I can follow a lecture" and indicate what they can do. Nunn (2000) provides very useful examples of rating scales for measuring learners' performance in small-group interaction. These scales are useful both for testing and for diagnostic analysis of learners' conversation skills.

Speaking Tests

The two main aspects of direct procedures for testing speaking are: (1) the way in which the person being tested is encouraged to speak (this can include being interviewed, having to describe something for someone to draw, being involved in a discussion etc.); and (2) the way in which the speaker's performance is assessed (this can include rating scales, communicative result, and assigning marks for the parts of an outcome). Due to the practical problems in measuring the speaking proficiency of large groups of people, there has been a continuing interest in more practicable indirect group measures.

Interviews and Scales

Each learner is interviewed individually. The interviewer does not need to follow a set series of questions but it is best to keep at least part of each interview as similar as possible. The interviewees are scored on rating scales from one to five for each of fluency, intelligibility, grammatical correctness, richness of language and overall impression (see Henning, 1983). As van Moere (2006) has shown, it is not easy to get good agreement between raters.

Group Oral Exam

The learners are divided into groups of four or five people. They are given a card with a topic and a few questions to think about. After a few moments thought the group discusses the topic. Two observers grade each learner using a set of scales (Folland and Robertson, 1976; Reves, 1982; Hilsdon, 1991). Instead of discussions, role plays, partly scripted dialogues, or partly improvised plays can be used to get the learners to speak (Hayward, 1983).

Dycoms (Split Information)

The learners are divided into two equal groups. All the people in group A have a sheet with 50 items on it like Figure 10.1. Those in group B have a slightly different sheet (Figure 10.2) (Nation, 1977).

Some of group B's items are exactly the same as the items on group A's sheet. Some are slightly different. The class forms pairs with someone from group A and someone from group B in each pair. The learners in each pair describe their items to each other and decide if they are the same or different. They must not show their pictures to each other. They write S next to the items that they decide are the same, and D next to the items that are different. After doing five items they change partners and do another five. This continues until they have had ten partners thus completing the 50 items. Each learner's paper is collected and marked. Their score out of 50 is a measure of their skill in communicating with ten different people (Byers, 1973). In tests where candidates are paired, who someone is paired with can affect the outcome of the assessment (Norton, 2005).

Describe and Draw

The learner is given a picture which they have to describe so that their partner, the examiner, can draw it. Marks are given for describing each part of the picture correctly with specific marks assigned for each part (Brown, Anderson, Shillcock and Yule, 1984; Politzer and McGroarty, 1983). In the test the examiner need not draw the item being described but can just assign the points for each part described successfully.

Conversational Cloze

This test does not involve any listening or speaking by learners. The learners are given a transcript of a conversation. Every seventh word is omitted from the transcript. The learners have to write in the missing words (Hughes, 1981; Brown, 1983). Brown (1983) found a high correlation of .84 between conversational cloze and oral interview tests. Other researchers have found similar correlations between cloze tests based on non-conversational texts and oral interview. There are problems in using indirect measures such as cloze in place of measures involving direct performance of the skill being measured. These include lack of diagnostic

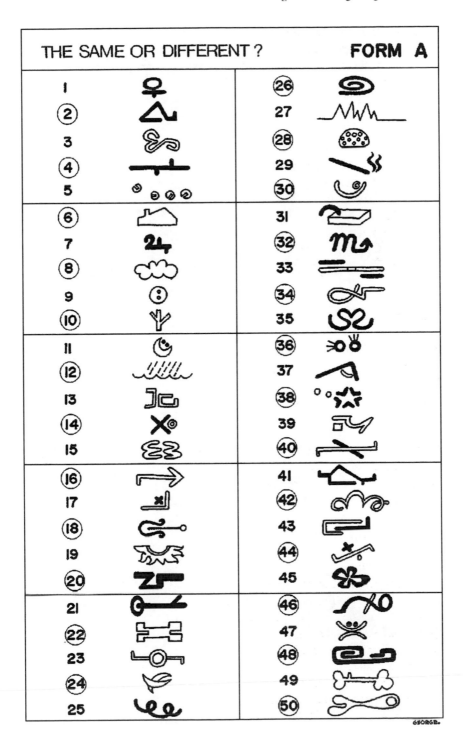

Figure 10.1 Split Information Sheet A

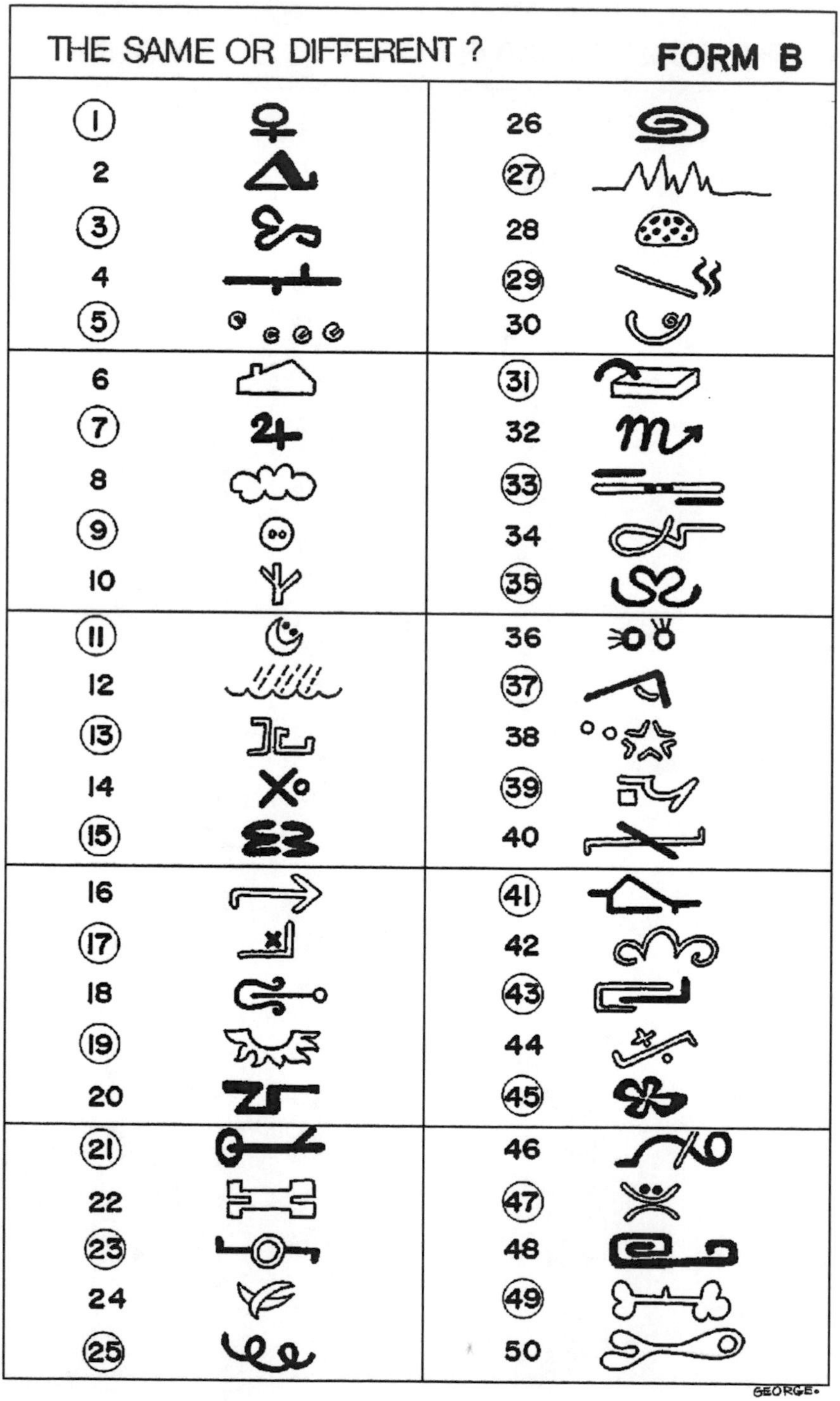

Figure 10.2 Split Information Sheet B

information, poor face validity, problems in interpreting scores, and the washback effect.

Multiple-choice Speaking Tests

The learners are given written multiple-choice items to answer. They do not speak during the test. Here is an example from Politzer and McGroarty (1983: 190).

> The students are taking a test and the teacher wants them to know that they can use their books. What are two ways that he could say this?
> A. Whose books are those?
> B. You may use your books for this test.
> C. Don't you know how to open your books?
> D. This is an open-book test.

Imitation

Learners listen to tape-recorded sentences of different lengths and repeat them. Usually a large number of sentences are used. Henning (1983) used 90 in his test. The sentences are judged as being correct or incorrect. A correct sentence is one that is repeated without any errors.

Role Plays

The learners are given a card which describes a situation. For example,

> You want to join an English course but you want to find out several things about the course before you make your final decision. Some of the things you want to know are the cost, the hours, the size of the groups. You are rather worried about being put in a large group where you will not get much individual attention.

The examiner also has a role to play.

> You are the course director. The course costs £150. There is an average of 14 people in a class. Classes are held from 9am to 3pm each week day with an hour for lunch. You want to make sure that anyone who does the course attends regularly.

After the role play the examiner scores the learner's performance on a set of scales. This procedure is particularly useful for testing English for specific purposes as the role plays can be suited to the jobs of the learners.

The choice of a format for testing speaking will depend on a range of factors including the proficiency level of the learners, their experience of various kinds of speaking activities, the reasons for testing, and how well the format satisfies the requirements of reliability, validity and practicality. Chapter 6 of the companion volume to this book, *Teaching ESL/EFL Reading and Writing*, looks more closely at the purposes for testing.

Conclusion

This book and its companion book, *Teaching ESL/EFL Reading and Writing*, are based on the idea that a well-balanced language course should consist of four strands. These are the strands of meaning-focused input, meaning-focused output, language-focused learning, and fluency development. Each of these strands provides different kinds of opportunity for learning and requires different conditions for the learning to occur. The meaning-focused input and the meaning-focused output strands have the conditions that the learners should be largely familiar with the language used in the strand and it should only contain a small amount of new material. This small amount of unknown language thus has an opportunity to be learnt because it is in a largely familiar supportive context. The language-focused learning strand involves deliberate learning. Learning in this strand is usually very efficient because learners are focused on what they should be learning and are aware of what they should be learning. The fluency development strand provides the opportunity to become really good at using what is already known. This strand requires that all of the material being worked with is familiar to the learners. In a well-balanced course each of these four strands has roughly the same amount of time.

Another way of looking at a course is to take a curriculum design approach. This typically involves looking at: (1) the situation in which the course occurs; (2) the needs of the learners; (3) the principles on which the course is based; (4) the goals of the course; (5) the content of the course; (6) the way in which the course is presented, that is, the activities which are used in the course and the format of the coursebook; (7) the monitoring and assessment used in the course; and, finally, (8) the evaluation of the course (Nation, 2000a). This book has largely focused on the way in which the course is presented, although some attention has been given to the principles which lie behind a course, the content of the course, and monitoring and assessment. Because this book is focused on the presentation of a course, a large number of teaching techniques have been described and justified. These techniques, however, have to be seen as providing opportunities for learning to take place or, to put it another way, as opportunities for putting principles into practice.

It is therefore important for teachers to develop the skill of looking at an activity while it is being used to see what signs there are that learning is occurring. An activity can involve the learners, keep them busy and interested, and yet have little learning value. Throughout this book we have looked at the conditions needed for the various strands. Meaning-focused input and output require a focus on the message, interest in the message, only a small amount of unfamiliar language features, a supportive context, and a friendly non-threatening learning environment. Language-focused learning requires deliberate attention to language features with the opportunity for repetition and thoughtful processing. Fluency development activities require a focus on the message, very easy material with no unfamiliar language items, pressure to go faster, and quantity of practise. When looking at activities, teachers need to note whether the learners are truly engaged with the material, but teachers also need to note whether the conditions needed for a particular strand are likely to be present or not. If they are not, then adjustments need to be made to bring them in.

This book has tried to provide a practical, principled introduction to the teaching of listening and speaking. Whenever possible it has based its suggestions and principles on research. This kind of book is one source of information for improving teaching and learning. Another important source is thoughtful and informed observation and reflection by teachers. We wish you well in that aspect of your development as a teacher.

Appendix 1: The Survival Syllabus

This appendix contains a language syllabus containing approximately 120 items which represents an easily achievable goal for people wishing to visit a foreign country for a month or more. The syllabus is the result of needs analyses involving interviews with learners, analysis of guide books, and personal experience. In addition, the items in the syllabus have been checked for frequency, coverage, and combinability. The syllabus is divided into eight categories: greetings and being polite; buying and bargaining; reading signs; getting to places; finding accommodation; ordering food; talking about yourself; and controlling and learning language. This list is intended for travellers making a short visit to another country. The full article is Crabbe, D. and Nation, P. (1991). A survival language learning syllabus for foreign travel. *System, 19*(3), 191–201. The Survival Syllabus is available in a variety of languages in the Vocabulary Rescue Book on Paul Nation's website.

The syllabus has been divided into eight sections on the basis of information revealed during the interviews. The sections have been ranked and numbered according to the number of interviewees indicating that they used items in the sections divided by the number of items. So the section *Greetings and being polite* was the most useful one. Items which occur in more than one section are indicated by numbers in brackets. So, *I want . . .* in Section 2 also occurs in Sections 5, 6, and 9. The slash (/) indicates alternatives.

1. *Greetings and Being Polite*

   Hello/Good morning etc. + reply [there are many cultural variants of these, including *Where are you going?, Have you eaten?*]
   How are you? + reply e.g. Fine, thank you.

Goodbye

Thank you + reply e.g. It's nothing, You're welcome.
Please

Excuse me [sorry]
It doesn't matter

Delicious (6)

Can I take your photo?

2. *Buying and Bargaining*

I want . . . (4, 6)
Do you have . . .?/Is there . . .?
Yes (8)
No (8)
This (one), That (one) [to use when pointing at goods]
There isn't any

How much (cost)? (5, 6)
A cheaper one (5)

NUMBERS (5, 7) (These need to be learned to a high degree of fluency)

UNITS OF MONEY (5, 6)

UNITS OF WEIGHT AND SIZE
How much (quantity)?
half
all of it
(one) more
(one) less

Excuse me [to get attention] (4)

Too expensive
Can you lower the price? + reply (Some countries do not use bargaining. In others it is essential.)

NAMES OF IMPORTANT THINGS TO BUY (These may include stamps, a newspaper, a map.)

3. *Reading Signs*

Gents
Ladies

Entrance/In

Exit/out
Closed

4. *Getting to Places*

Excuse me (to get attention) (2)
Can you help me?

Where is . . .? (5)
Where is . . . street?
What is the name of this place/street/station/town?

Toilet
Bank
Department store
Restaurant
Airport
Train station
Underground
Bus station
Hospital
Doctor
Police
Post-office
Telephone
Market
I want . . . (2, 5, 6)

How far?/Is it near?
How long (to get to . . .)?

Left
Right
Straight ahead
Slow down (Directions for a taxi.)
Stop here
Wait

Ticket

When

5. *Finding Accommodation*

Where is . . . (4)
Hotel

How much (cost)? (2, 6)
A cheaper one (2)

I want . . . (2, 4, 6)

Leave at what time?
NUMBERS (2, 7)
today
tomorrow

6. *Ordering Food*

How much (cost)? (2, 5)
The bill, please

I want . . . (2, 5, 9)

NAMES OF A FEW DISHES AND DRINKS

A FEW COOKING TERMS

Delicious (1)

7. *Talking about Yourself and Talking to Children*
I am (name)
Where do you come from?
I am (an American)/I come from (America)

What do you do?

I am a (teacher)/tourist

You speak (Chinese)!
A little/very little

What is your name? (Especially for talking to children.)
How old are you? + reply
NUMBERS (2, 5)

I have been here . . . days/weeks/months

I am sick

8. *Controlling and Learning Language*
Do you understand?
I (don't) understand
Do you speak English? (7)
Yes (2)
No (2)

Repeat
Please speak slowly
I speak only a little (Thai)

What do you call this in (Japanese)?

Appendix 2: Topic Types

Johns and Davies (1983) described 12 topic types. Some are much more common than others. The following list is adapted from Johns and Davies and lists the most important topic types and their parts. The topic type hypothesis is that texts on different topics but which are all of the same topic type will contain the same general kinds of information.

The Most Useful Topic Types and Their Parts

Characteristics

What are the features of the thing described?
What is the proof that some of these features exist?
What general category does this thing fit into?
What other information is there about this thing?

Physical Structure

What are the parts?
Where are the parts located?
What are they like?
What do they do?

Instruction

What are the steps involved?
What materials and equipment are needed?
What do we need to be careful about at some steps?

What is the result of the steps?
What does this result show?

Process

What are the stages involved in the development?
What material is involved at each stage?
Where and when does each stage occur?
How long does each stage last?
What acts at each stage to bring about change?
What is the thing like at each stage?
What happens at each stage?

State/Situation

Who are the people etc. involved?
What time and place are involved?
What is the background leading up to the happening?
What happened?
What are the effects of this happening?

Principle

What is the law or principle involved?
Under what conditions does the principle apply?
What are some examples of the principle in action?
How can we check to see that the principle is in action?
How can we apply the principle?

Theory

What is the hypothesis?
What led to this hypothesis?
How is it tested?
What are the results of testing?
What is the significance of the results?

Appendix 3: Topics for Listening and Speaking

Giving Information About Yourself and Your Family

Asking Others for Similar Information

- name
- address
- phone
- partner and family
- length of residence
- origin
- job
- age

Meeting People

- greetings
- talking about the weather
- inviting for a meal etc.
- telling the time and day
- saying what you like
- saying you are sorry
- joining a club

Going Shopping

- finding goods
- asking for a quantity
- understanding prices

Using Important Services

- post office
- bank
- public telephone
- police
- garage

Asking How to Get to Places

Telling Others Directions

- directions
- distance and time
- using public transport

Taking Care of Your Health

- contacting a doctor
- reporting illness
- describing previous illness and medical conditions
- calling emergency services

Describing Your Home, Town, and Country

Asking Others for Similar Information

- house\flat
- features of the town
- features of your country
- furniture

Describing Your Job

Asking Others about their Job

- job
- place
- conditions
- travelling to work

Finding out How to Get a Job

- kind of job
- where to look
- what to do

Finding Food and Drink

- getting attention
- using a menu
- ordering a meal
- offering food
- praising the food
- finding a toilet
- giving thanks

Taking Part in Sport and Entertainment

- saying when you are free
- buying tickets
- say what you like and do not like doing

Special Needs

References

Abbott, G. 1986. A new look at phonological "redundancy". *ELT Journal* 40, 4: 299–305.

Acton, W. 1984. Changing fossilized pronunciation. *TESOL Quarterly* 18, 1: 71–85.

Allen, R.L. 1972. The use of rapid drills in the teaching of English to speakers of other languages. *TESOL Quarterly* 6, 1: 13–32.

Anderson, A. and Lynch, T. 1988. *Listening*. Oxford: Oxford University Press.

Anderson, J.R. 1989. Practice, working memory, and the ACT* theory of skill acquisition: a comment on Carlson, Sullivan, and Schneider. *Journal of Experimental Psychology: Learning Memory, and Cognition* 15: 527–530.

Arevart, S. and Nation, I.S.P. 1991. Fluency improvement in a second language. *RELC Journal* 22, 1: 84–94.

Asher, J.J., Kosudo, J.A. and De La Torre, R. 1974. Learning a second language through commands: the second field test. *Modern Language Journal* 58, 1–2: 24–32.

Aston, G. 1986. Trouble-shooting in interaction with learners: the more the merrier? *Applied Linguistics* 7, 2: 128–143.

Atkins, P.W.B. and Baddeley, A. 1998. Working memory and distributed vocabulary learning. *Applied Psycholinguistics* 19: 537–552.

Aufderhaar, C. 2004. Learner views of using authentic audio to aid pronunciation: "You can just grab some feelings". *TESOL Quarterly* 38, 4: 735–746.

Baddeley, A. 1990. *Human Memory*. Hillsdale: Lawrence Erlbaum Associates.

Baddeley, A., Gathercole, S. and Papagno, C. 1998. The phonological loop as a language learning device. *Psychological Review* 105, 1: 158–173.

Badger, R. 1986. Grids. *English Teaching Forum* 24, 4: 36–38.

Barnett, J.E., Di Vesta, F.J. and Rogoszinski, J.T. 1981. What is learned in note-taking? *Journal of Educational Psychology* 73, 2: 181–192.

Bauer, L. and Nation, I.S.P. 1993. Word families. *International Journal of Lexicography* 6, 4: 253–279.

Biber, D. 1989. A typology of English texts. *Linguistics* 27: 3–43.

Biber, D., Johansson, S., Leech, G., Conrad, S. and Finegan, E. 1999. *Longman Grammar of Spoken and Written English*. Harlow: Longman.

Bismoko, J. and Nation, I.S.P. 1974. English reading speed and the mother-tongue or national language. *RELC Journal* 5, 1: 86–89.

Bligh, D. 1972. *What's the Use of Lectures?* Harmondsworth: Penguin.

Boers, F., Eyckmans, J., Kappel, J., Stengers, H. and Demecheleer, M. 2006. Formulaic sequences and perceived oral proficiency: putting the Lexical Approach to the test. *Language Teaching Research* 10, 3: 245–261.

Breitkreuz, H. 1972. Picture stories in language teaching. *ELT Journal* 26, 2: 145–149.

Briere, E.J. 1967. Phonological testing reconsidered. *Language Learning* 17, 3 and 4: 163–171.

Briere, E.J. 1968. *A Psycholinguistic Study of Phonological Interference.* The Hague: Mouton.

Brown, A. 1989. Models, standards, targets/goals and norms in pronunciation teaching. *World Englishes* 8, 2: 193–200.

Brown, D. 1983. Conversational cloze tests and conversational ability. *ELT Journal* 37, 2: 158–161.

Brown, D. and Barnard, H. 1975. Dictation as a learning experience. *RELC Journal* 6, 2: 42–62.

Brown, G. 1978. Understanding spoken language. *TESOL Quarterly* 12, 3: 271–283.

Brown, G. 1981. Teaching the spoken language. *Studia Linguistica* 35, 1–2: 166–182.

Brown, G. 1982. Teaching and assessing spoken language. *TESL Talk* 13, 3: 3–13.

Brown, G. 1986. Investigating listening comprehension in context. *Applied Linguistics* 7, 3: 284–302.

Brown, G., Anderson, A., Shillcock, R. and Yule, G. 1984. *Teaching Talk.* Cambridge: Cambridge University Press.

Brown, H.D. 1993. Requiem for methods. *Journal of Intensive English Studies* 7: 1–12.

Brown, J. 1979. Vocabulary: Learning to be imprecise. *Modern English Teacher* 7, 1: 25–27.

Brumfit, C.J. 1984. *Communicative Methodology in Language Teaching: The roles of fluency and accuracy.* Cambridge: Cambridge University Press.

Brumfit, C.J. 1985. Accuracy and fluency: a fundamental distinction for communicative teaching methodology. In C.J. Brumfit, *Language and Literature Teaching: From Practice to Principle*, Oxford: Pergamon.

Buckeridge, D. 1988. "Ask 'n' move"—a role play for elementary students. *Modern English Teacher* 15, 2: 24–26.

Burton, D. 1986. The odd man out. *Modern English Teacher* 13, 4: 43–44.

Buzan, T. 1974. *Use Your Head.* London: BBC.

Byers, B.H. 1973. Testing proficiency in interpersonal communication. *RELC Journal* 4, 2: 39–47.

Bygate, M. 1988. Units of oral expression and language learning in small group interaction. *Applied Linguistics* 9, 1: 59–82.

Cabrera, M. and Martinez, P. 2001. The effects of repetition, comprehension checks, and gestures on primary school children in an EFL situation. *ELT Journal* 55, 3: 281–288.

Carr, E.B. 1967. Teaching the *th* sounds of English. *TESOL Quarterly* 1, 1: 7–14.

Cheng, P.W. 1985. Restructuring versus automaticity: alternative accounts of skill acquisition. *Psychological Review* 92: 414–423.

Chung, M. and Nation, I.S.P. 2006. The effect of a speed reading course. *English Teaching* 61, 4: 181–204.

Clarke, D.F. 1991. The negotiated syllabus: what is it and how is it likely to work? *Applied Linguistics* 12, 1: 13–28.

Clennell, C. 1999. Promoting pragmatic awareness and spoken discourse skills with EAP classes. *ELT Journal* 53, 2: 83–91.

Coe, N. 1972. What use are songs in FL teaching? *IRAL* 10, 4: 357–360.

Cole, P. 1972. Some techniques for communication practice. *English Teaching Forum* 10, 1: 2–5, 20.

Coughlan, P. and Duff, P. 1994. Same task, different activities: Analysis of SLA from an activity theory perspective. In J. Lantolf and G. Appel (eds), *Vygotskian Approaches to Second Language Research* (pp. 173–194). Norwood, NJ: Ablex.

Coxhead, A. 2000. A new academic word list. *TESOL Quarterly* 34, 2: 213–238.

Crabbe, D. and Nation, I.S.P. 1991. A survival language learning syllabus for foreign travel. *System* 19, 3: 191–201.

Craik, F. I. M. and Lockhart, R. S. 1972. Levels of processing: a framework for memory research. *Journal of Verbal Learning and Verbal Behaviour* 11: 671–684.

Craik, F.I.M. and Tulving, E. 1975. Depth of processing and the retention of words in episodic memory. *Journal of Experimental Psychology* 104: 268–284.

Cramer, S. 1975. Increasing reading speed in English or in the national language. *RELC Journal* 6, 2: 19–23.

Crookes, G. 1989. Planning and interlanguage variation. *SSLA* 11: 367–384.

Cunningham, A.E. and Stanovich, K.E. 1991. Tracking the unique effects of print exposure in children: associations with vocabulary, general knowledge, and spelling. *Journal of Educational Psychology* 83, 2: 264–274.

Dauer, R.M. 1983. Stress-timing and syllable-timing reanalysed. *Journal of Phonetics* 11: 51–62.

Davidson, D. 1980. Vevir and the python. *School Journal* Part 2, Number 1: 36–39.

Davies, A. 1990. *Principles of Language Testing.* Oxford: Basil Blackwell.

Day, R. 1981. Silence and the ESL child. *TESOL Quarterly* 15, 1: 35–39.

DeKeyser, R. 2007. Introduction: situating the concept of practice. In R. DeKeyser (ed.), *Practice in a Second Language* (pp. 1–18). Cambridge: Cambridge University Press.

Denham, P. A. 1974. Design and three-item paradigms. *ELT Journal* 28, 2: 138–145.

Derwing, T. and Munro, M. 2005. Second language accent and pronunciation teaching: a research-based approach. *TESOL Quarterly* 39, 3: 379–398.

Deyes, A.F. 1973. Language games for advanced students. *ELT Journal* 27, 2: 160–165.

Dickerson, W.B. 1990. Morphology via orthography: a visual approach to oral decisions. *Applied Linguistics* 11, 3: 238–252.

Dobbyn, M. 1976. An objective test of pronunciation for large classes. *ELT Journal* 30, 3: 242–244.

Doughty, C. 2003. Instructed SLA: constraints, compensation, and enhancement. In C. Doughty and M. H. Long (eds), *The Handbook of Second Language Acquisition* (pp. 256–310). Malden, MA: Blackwell.

Doughty, C. and Williams, J. (eds). 1998. *Focus on Form in Classroom Second Language Acquisition.* Cambridge: Cambridge University Press.

Doyle, W. 1983. Academic work. *Review of Educational Research* 53, 2: 159–199.

Dunn, A. 1993. Dictogloss—When the words get in the way. *TESOL in Context* 8, 2: 21–23.

Duppenthaler, P. 1988. Hints. *English Teaching Forum* 26, 3: 46.

Dupuy, B. 1999. Narrow listening: An alternative way to develop listening comprehension in the foreign language classroom. *System* 24, 1: 97–100.

Dušková, L. 1969. On sources of errors in foreign language learning. *IRAL* 7: 11–36.

Eckman, F.R., Bell, L. and Nelson, D. 1988. On the generalisation of relative clause instruction in the acquisition of English as a second language. *Applied Linguistics* 9, 1: 1–20.

Elgort, I. 2007. The role of intentional decontextualised learning in second language vocabulary acquisition: evidence from primed lexical decision tasks with advanced bilinguals. Unpublished PhD thesis, Victoria University of Wellington, New Zealand.

Elkins, R.J., Kalivoda, T.B. and Morain, G. 1972. Fusion of the four skills: a technique for facilitating communicative exchange. *Modern Language Journal* 56, 7: 426–429.

Elley, W.B. 1989. Vocabulary acquisition from listening to stories. *Reading Research Quarterly* 24, 2: 174–187.

Elley, W.B. and Mangubhai, F. 1981. *The Impact of a Book Flood in Fiji Primary Schools.* Wellington: NZCER.

Ellis, N. C. and Beaton, A. 1993. Psycholinguistic determinants of foreign language vocabulary learning. *Language Learning* 43, 4: 559–617.

Ellis, R. 1986. *Understanding Second Language Acquisition.* Oxford: Oxford University Press.

Ellis, R. 1990. *Instructed Second Language Acquisition.* Oxford: Basil Blackwell.

Ellis, R. 1991. The interaction hypothesis: a critical evaluation. In E. Sadtono (ed.) *Language Acquisition and the Second/Foreign Language Classroom.* RELC Anthology Series 28: 179–211.

Ellis, R. 1992. Learning to communicate in the classroom: a study of two language learners' requests. *SSLA* 14, 1: 1–23.

Ellis, R. 2002. The place of grammar instruction in the second/foreign language curriculum. In E. Hinkel and S. Fotos (eds), *New Perspectives on Grammar Teaching in Second Language Classrooms* (pp. 13–34). Mahwah, NJ: Lawrence Erlbaum.

Ellis, R. 2005. Principles of instructed language learning. *System* 33: 209–224.

Ellis, R. 2006. Current issues in the teaching of grammar: an SLA perspective. *TESOL Quarterly* 40, 1: 83–107.

Emery, P. 1980. Evaluating spoken English: a new approach to the testing of listening comprehension. *ELT Journal* 34, 2: 96–98.

Esling, J.H. and Wong, R.F. 1983. Voice quality settings and the teaching of pronunciation. *TESOL Quarterly* 17, 1: 89–95.

Farid, A. 1978. Developing the listening and speaking skills: a suggested procedure. *ELT Journal* 33, 1: 27–30.

Field, J. 2000. "Not waving but drowning": a reply to Tony Ridgway. *ELT Journal* 54, 2: 186–195.

Field, J. 2003. Promoting perception: lexical segmentation in L2 listening. *ELT Journal* 57, 4: 325–334.

Flege, J.E. 1981. The phonological basis of foreign accent: a hypothesis. *TESOL Quarterly* 15, 4: 443–455.

Flege, J.E. 1987. A critical period for learning to pronounce foreign languages. *Applied Linguistics* 8, 2: 162–177.

Flege, J.E. and Port, R. 1981. Cross-language phonetic interference: Arabic to English. *Language and Speech* 24: 125–146.

Flenley, T. 1982. Making realistic listening material. *Modern English Teacher* 10, 2: 14–15.

Folland, D. and Robertson, D. 1976. Towards objectivity in group oral testing. *ELT Journal* 30, 2: 156–167.

Folse, K. 1991. Could you repeat that? An innovative way of getting students to speak up. *TESL Reporter* 24, 2: 23–25.

Fotos, S.F. 1993. Conscious raising and noticing through focus on form: grammar task performance versus formal instruction. *Applied Linguistics* 14, 4: 385–407.

Fotos, S. 2002. Structure-based interactive tasks. In E. Hinkel and S. Fotos (eds), *New Perspectives on Grammar Teaching in Second Language Classrooms* (pp. 181–198). Mahwah, NJ: Lawrence Erlbaum.

Fotos, S. and Ellis, R. 1991. Communicating about grammar: a task-based approach. *TESOL Quarterly* 25, 4: 605–628.

Fowles, J. 1970. Ho! Ho! Ho! Cartoons in the language classroom. *TESOL Quarterly* 4, 2: 155–159.

Franken, M. 1987. Self-questioning scales for improving academic writing. *Guidelines* 9, 1: 1–8.

Gary, J.D. and Gary, N.G. 1981. Caution: talking may be dangerous for your linguistic health. *IRAL* 19, 1: 1–13.

Gass, S. 1997. *Input, Interaction and the Second Language Learner*. Mahwah, NJ: Lawrence Erlbaum.

George, H.V. 1963. *Report on a Verb Form Frequency Count*. Monograph of the Central Institute of English, Hyderabad (No. 1 and No. 2).

George, H.V. 1965. The substitution table. *ELT Journal* 20, 1: 46–48.

George, H.V. 1972. *Common Errors in Language Learning*. Rowley, Mass.: Newbury House.

George, H.V. 1990. Listening skills. *Guidelines* 12, 1: 14–25.

George, H.V. and Neo, B.C. 1974. A theory of stress. *RELC Journal* 5, 1: 50–63.

Gibson, R.E. 1975. The strip story: a catalyst for communication. *TESOL Quarterly* 9, 2: 149–154.

Givon, T., Yang, L. and Gernsbacher, M.A. 1990. The processing of second language vocabulary: from attended to automated word-recognition. In H. Burmeister and P.L. Rounds (eds), *Variability in Second Language Acquisition*. Vol.1. Department of Linguistics, University of Oregon.

Goh, C. 2000. A cognitive perspective on language learners' listening comprehension problems. *System* 28, 1: 55–75.

Gower, R. 1981. Structured conversations. *Modern English Teacher* 9, 1: 27–29. 2: 141–150.

Green, K. 1975. Values clarification theory in ESL and bilingual education. *TESOL Quarterly* 9, 2: 155–164.

Gregg, K. R. 1984. Krashen's monitor and Occam's razor. *Applied Linguistics* 5: 79–100.

Griffin, G.F. and Harley, T.A. 1996. List learning of second language vocabulary. *Applied Psycholinguistics* 17: 443–460.

Griffiths, R. 1991a. Language classroom speech rates: a descriptive study. *TESOL Quarterly* 25, 1: 189–194.

Griffiths, R. 1991b. Pausological research in an L2 context: a rationale, and review of selected studies. *Applied Linguistics* 12, 4: 345–364.

Guiora, A.Z., Beit-Hallami, B., Brannon, R.C.L., Dull, C.Y. and Scovel, T. 1972a. The effects of experimentally induced changes in ego states on pronunciation ability in a second language: an exploratory study. *Comprehensive Psychiatry* 13: 421–428.

Guiora, A.Z., Brannon, R.C.L. and Dull, C.Y. 1972b. Empathy and second language learning. *Language Learning* 22, 1: 111–130.

Gurrey, P. 1955. *Teaching English as a Foreign Language*. London: Longman.

Hall, R. W. 1971. Ann and Abby: the agony column on the air. *TESOL Quarterly* 5, 3: 247–249.

Halverson, J. 1967. Stress, pitch, and juncture. *ELT Journal* 21, 3: 210–217.

Hammerly, H. 1982. Contrastive phonology and error analysis. *IRAL* 20, 1: 17–32.

Hamp-Lyons, L. 1983. Survey of materials for teaching advanced listening and notetaking. *TESOL Quarterly* 17, 1: 109–122.

Harris, D.P. 1970. Report on an experimental group administered memory span test. *TESOL Quarterly* 4, 3: 203–213.

Hayward, T. 1983. Passive assessor tests: an alternative to interviews for assessing communicative performance in spoken English. *World Language English* 3, 1: 39–43.

Hendrickson, J.M. 1978. Error correction in foreign language teaching: recent theory, research and practice. *Modern Language Journal* 62, 8: 387–398.

Henning, G. 1983. Oral proficiency testing: comparative validities of interview, imitation, and completion methods. *Language Learning* 33, 3: 315–332.

Henning, W.A. 1966. Discrimination training and self-evaluation in the teaching of pronunciation. *IRAL* 4, 1: 7–17.

Herman, P.A., Anderson, R.C., Pearson, P.D. and Nagy, W.E. 1987. Incidental acquisition of word meaning from expositions with varied text features. *Reading Research Quarterly* 22, 3: 263–284.

Higa, M. 1963. Interference effects of interlist word relationships in verbal learning. *Journal of Verbal Learning and Verbal Behavior* 2: 170–175.

Hill, L.A. 1969. Delayed copying. *ELT Journal* 23, 3: 238–239.

Hill, M. and Storey, A. 2003. *SpeakEasy*: online support for oral presentation skills. *ELT Journal* 57, 4: 370–376.

Hilsdon, J. 1991. The group oral exam: advantages and limitations. In J.C. Alderson and B. North (eds), *Language Testing in the 1990s: the Communicative Legacy*. London: Macmillan.

Hinkel, E. 2006. Current perspectives on teaching the four skills. *TESOL Quarterly* 40, 1: 109–131.

Hirvela, A. 1987. Extended story-telling. *Modern English Teacher* 14, 3: 18–21.

Hole, J. 1983. Pronunciation testing—What did you say? *ELT Journal* 37, 2: 127–128.

Holmes, J. and Brown, D.F. 1976. Developing sociolinguistic competence in a second language. *TESOL Quarterly* 10, 4: 423–431.

Hu, M. and Nation, I.S.P. 2000. Unknown vocabulary density and reading comprehension. *Reading in a Foreign Language* 13, 1: 403–430.

Hughes, A. 1981. Conversational cloze as a measure of oral ability. *ELT Journal* 35, 2: 161–167.

Hughes, G.S. 1985. Positioning: drama and communication. *English Teaching Forum* 23, 3: 40–41.

Ilson, R. 1962. The dicto-comp: a specialized technique for controlling speech and writing in language learning. *Language Learning* 12, 4: 299–301.

Ingram, D. 1981. The Australian second language proficiency ratings. In J.A.S. Read (ed.), *Directions in Language Teaching*, RELC Anthology Series 3: 108–136.

Ingram, D. 1984. *Australian second language proficiency ratings.* Department of Immigration and Ethnic Affairs, Canberra.

Izumi, S. 2002. Output, input enhancement, and the noticing hypothesis: an experimental study on ESL relativization. *SSLA* 24, 541–577.

Jenkins, J. 2002. A sociolinguistically based, empirically researched pronunciation syllabus for English as an international language. *Applied Linguistics* 23, 1: 83–103.

Jenkins, J.R., Stein, M.L. and Wysocki, K. 1984. Learning vocabulary through reading. *American Educational Research Journal* 21, 4: 767–787.

Joe, A. 1998. What effects do text-based tasks promoting generation have on incidental vocabulary acquisition? *Applied Linguistics* 19, 357–377.

Joe, A., Nation, P. and Newton, J. 1996. Vocabulary learning and speaking activities. *English Teaching Forum* 34, 1: 2–7.

Johns, T. and Davies, F. 1983. Text as a vehicle for information: the classroom use of written texts in teaching reading in a foreign language. *Reading in a Foreign Language* 1, 1: 1–19.

Johnson, K. 1988. Mistake correction. *ELT Journal* 42, 2: 89–96.

Jones, D. 1960. *An Outline of English Phonetics.* Cambridge: Heffer, 9th edn.

Jones, R.E. 2001. A consciousness-raising approach to the teaching of conversational story-telling skills. *ELT Journal* 55, 2: 155–163.

Jordan, R.R. 1990. Pyramid discussions. *ELT Journal* 44, 1: 46–54.

Joycey, E. 1982. Group work, the information gap and the individual. *Modern English Teacher* 10, 1: 25–26.

Kellerman, S. 1990. Lip service: the contribution of the visual modality to speech perception and its relevance to the teaching and testing of foreign language listening comprehension. *Applied Linguistics* 11, 3: 272–280.

Krahnke, K.J. and Christison, M.A. 1983. Recent language research and some language teaching principles. *TESOL Quarterly* 17, 4: 625–649.

Krashen, S.D. 1981. The "fundamental pedagogical principle" in second language teaching. *Studia Linguistica* 35, 1–2: 50–70.

Krashen, S.D. 1985. *The Input Hypothesis: Issues and Implications.* London: Longman.

Kuhn, M. and Stahl, S. 2003. Fluency: a review of developmental and remedial practices. *Journal of Educational Psychology* 95, 1: 3–21.

Lado, R. 1965. Memory span as a factor in second language learning. *IRAL* 3, 2: 123–129.

Larsen-Freeman, D. and Long, M.H. 1991. *An Introduction to Second Language Acquisition Research.* London: Longman.

Leeman, J. 2007. Feedback in L2 learning: responding to errors during practice. In R. DeKeyser (ed.), *Practice in a Second Language* (pp. 111–137). Cambridge: Cambridge University Press.

Lennon, P. 1990. Investigating fluency in EFL: a quantitative approach. *Language Learning* 40, 3: 387–417.

Lennon, P. 1991. Error: some problems of definition, identification, and distinction. *Applied Linguistics* 12, 2: 180–196.

Leung, C. and Lewkowicz, J. 2006. Expanding horizons and unresolved conundrums: language testing and assessment. *TESOL Quarterly* 40, 1: 211–234.

Levis, J. 2005. Changing contexts and shifting paradigms in pronunciation teaching. *TESOL Quarterly* 39, 3: 369–377.

Lewis, M. 1993. *The Lexical Approach.* Hove: Language Teaching Publications.

Locke, J. L. 1970. The value of repetition in articulation learning. *IRAL* 8, 2: 147–154.

Long, M. H. 1996. The role of the linguistic environment in second language acquisition. In W. C. Ritchie and T. K. Bhatia (eds), *Handbook of Language Acquisition* (Vol. 2: Second Language Acquisition, pp. 413–468). New York: Academic Press.

Long, M. 1988. Instructed interlanguage development. In L. Beebe (ed.), *Issues in Second Language Acquisition.* New York: Newbury House.

Lynch, T. 2001. Seeing what they meant: transcribing as a route to noticing. *ELT Journal* 55, 2: 124–132.

Lynch, T. and Mendelsohn, D. 2002. Listening. In N. Schmitt (ed.), *An Introduction to Applied Linguistics* (pp. 193–210). London: Arnold.

Mackey, A. 1999. Input, interaction, and second language development. *SSLA* 21: 557–587.

Mackey, A. 2007. Interaction as practice. In R. DeKeyser (ed.), *Practice in a Second Language* (pp. 85–110). Cambridge: Cambridge University Press.

Major, R.C. 1987. Foreign accent: recent research and theory. *IRAL* 25, 3: 185–202.

Maurice, K. 1983. The fluency workshop. *TESOL Newsletter* 17, 4: 29.

Mayo, M. 2002. The effectiveness of two form-focused tasks in advanced EFL pedagogy. *International Journal of Applied Linguistics* 12, 2: 156–175.

McCarthy, M. and Carter, R. 2003. What constitutes a basic spoken vocabulary? *Research Notes: Cambridge University Press* (www.CambridgeESOL.org/researchnotes/), August, 5–7.

McComish, J. 1982. Listening to pictures. *Modern English Teacher* 10, 2: 4–8.

McKay, H. and Tom, A. 1999. *Teaching Adult Second Language Learners.* Cambridge: Cambridge University Press.

Mennim, P. 2003. Rehearsed oral L2 output and reactive focus on form. *ELT Journal* 57, 2: 130–138.

Messer, S. 1967. Implicit phonology in children. *Journal of Verbal Learning and Verbal Behavior* 6: 609–613.

Mhone, Y.W. 1988. . . . It's my word, teacher! *English Teaching Forum* 26, 2: 48–51.

Munby, J. 1978. *Communicative Syllabus Design.* Cambridge: Cambridge University Press.

Nakahama, Y., Tyler, A. and van Lier, L. 2001. Negotiation of meaning in conversational and information gap activities: A comparative discourse analysis. *TESOL Quarterly* 35: 377–405.

Nation, I.S.P. 1975. Motivation, repetition and language teaching techniques. *ELT Journal* 29, 2: 115–120.

Nation, I.S.P. 1977. The combining arrangement: some techniques. *Modern Language Journal* 61, 3: 89–94.

Nation, I.S.P. 1978. "What is it?" a multipurpose language teaching technique. *English Teaching Forum* 16,3: 20–23, 32.

Nation, I.S.P. 1980. Graded interviews for communicative practice. *English Teaching Forum* 18, 4: 26–29.

Nation, I.S.P. 1988. Using techniques well: information transfer. *Guidelines* 10, 1: 17–23.

Nation, I.S.P. 1989a. Improving speaking fluency. *System* 17, 3: 377–384.

Nation, I.S.P. 1989b. Group work and language learning. *English Teaching Forum* 27: 2: 20–24.

Nation, I.S.P. 1990. *Teaching and Learning Vocabulary.* New York: Newbury House.

Nation, I.S.P. 1993. Sixteen principles of language teaching. In L. Bauer and C. Franzen (eds), *Of Pavlova, Poetry and Paradigms: Essays in Honour of Harry Orsman* (pp. 209–224). Wellington: Victoria University Press.

Nation, I.S.P. 2000a. Designing and improving a language course. *English Teaching Forum* 38, 4: 2–11.

Nation, I.S.P. 2000b. Learning vocabulary in lexical sets: dangers and guidelines. *TESOL Journal* 9, 2: 6–10.

Nation, I.S.P. 2001. *Learning Vocabulary in Another Language.* Cambridge: Cambridge University Press.

Nation, I.S.P. 2006. How large a vocabulary is needed for reading and listening? *Canadian Modern Language Review*, 63, 1: 59–82.

Nation, I.S.P. 2008. *Teaching Vocabulary: Strategies and Techniques.* Boston: Heinle Cengage Learning.

Nation, I.S.P. 2009. *Teaching ESL/EFL Reading and Writing.* New York: Routledge, Taylor and Francis.

Nation, P. and Wang, K. 1999. Graded readers and vocabulary. *Reading in a Foreign Language* 12, 2: 355–380.

Newmark, L. 1981. Participatory observation: how to succeed in language learning. In H. Winitz (ed.), *The Comprehension Approach to Foreign Language Instruction.* Rowley, Mass.: Newbury House.

Newton, J. 1995. Task-based interaction and incidental vocabulary learning: a case study. *Second Language Research* 11, 2: 159–177.

Nord, J.R. 1980. Developing listening fluency before speaking: an alternative paradigm. *System* 8 1: 1–22.

Norton, J. 2005. The paired format in the Cambridge Speaking Tests. *ELT Journal* 59, 4: 287–297.

Nunan, D. 1998. Approaches to teaching listening in the language classroom. In *Proceedings of the 1997 Korea TESOL Conference. Taejon, Korea: KOTESOL.* http://www.kotesol.org/publications/proceedings/1997/nunan_david.pdf (html version) (retrieved 15 November 2007).

Nunn, R. 2000. Designing rating scales for small-group interaction. *ELT Journal* 54, 2: 169–178.

Ohta, A. 2005. Interlanguage pragmatics in the zone of proximal development. *System* 33, 3: 503–517.

Oller, J. 1979. *Language Tests at School.* London: Longman.

Oller, J. W. and Streiff, V. 1975. Dictation: a test of grammar-based expectancies. *ELT Journal* 30, 1: 25–36.

Ortega, L. 1999. Planning and focus on form in L2 oral performance. *SSLA* 21, 1: 109–148.

Palka, E. 1981. A structure conversion game. *Modern English Teacher* 8, 4: 14–16.

Palmer, D.M. 1982. Information transfer for listening and reading. *English Teaching Forum* 20, 1: 29–33.

Palmer, H. 1925. Conversation. In R.C. Smith (ed.) 1999. *The Writings of Harold E. Palmer: An Overview* (pp. 185–191). Tokyo: Hon-no-Tomosha.

Papagno, C., Valentine, T. and Baddeley, A. 1991. Phonological short-term memory and foreign-language vocabulary learning. *Journal of Memory and Language* 30: 331–347.

Patowski, M. 1990. Age and accent in a second language: a reply to James Emil Flege. *Applied Linguistics* 11: 73–89.

Pennington, M.C. and Richards, J.C. 1986. Pronunciation revisited. *TESOL Quarterly* 20, 2: 207–225.

Pica, T., Holliday, L., Lewis, N. and Morgenthaler, L. 1989. Comprehensible output as an outcome of linguistics demands on the learner. *SSLA* 11, 63–90.

Picken, J. 1988. Let the students judge. *Modern English Teacher* 15, 4: 39–41.

Pienemann, M. 2003. Language processing capacity. In C. Doughty and M. H. Long (eds), *The Handbook of Second Language Acquisition* (pp. 679–714). Malden, MA: Blackwell.

Pike, K. L. 1947. *Phonemics.* Ann Arbor: University of Michigan Press.

Politzer, R. and McGroarty, M. 1983. A discrete point test of communicative competence. *IRAL* 21, 3: 180–191.

Purcell, E.T. and Suter, R.W. 1980. Predictors of pronunciation accuracy: a re-examination. *Language Learning* 30, 2: 271–287.

Purvis, K. 1983. The teacher as moderator: a technique for interactional learning. *ELT Journal* 37, 3: 221–228.

Reves, T. 1982. The group-oral examination: a field experiment. *World Language English* 1, 4: 259–262.

Richards, J.C. 1969. Songs in language learning. *TESOL Quarterly* 3, 2: 161–174.

Richards, J.C. 1974. *Error Analysis: Perspectives on Second Language Acquisition.* London: Longman.

Richards, J.C. 1990. *The Language Teaching Matrix.* Cambridge: Cambridge University Press.
Ridgway, T. 2000a. Listening strategies—I beg your pardon? *ELT Journal* 54, 2: 179–185.
Ridgway, T. 2000b. Hang on a minute! *ELT Journal* 54, 2: 196–197.
Riley, P.M. 1972. The dicto-comp. *English Teaching Forum* 10, 1: 21–23.
Robinett, B. W. 1965. Simple classroom techniques for teaching pronunciation. *On Teaching English to Speakers of Other Languages* NCTE: 135–138.
Rost, M. 2002. *Teaching and Researching Listening.* London: Pearson.
Rubin, J. 1994. A review of second language listening comprehension research. *Modern Language Journal* 78, 2: 199–221.
Sawyer, J and Silver, S. 1961. Dictation in language learning. *Language Learning* 11, 1 and 2: 33–42.
Sayer, P. 2005. An intensive approach to building conversation skills. *ELT Journal* 59, 1: 14–22.
Schmidt, R.W. 1992. Psychological mechanisms underlying second language fluency. *SSLA* 14: 357–385.
Schmitt, N. and Meara, P. 1997. Researching vocabulary through a word knowledge framework: word associations and verbal suffixes. *SSLA* 19, 17–36.
Seedhouse, P. 1999. Task-based interaction. *ELT Journal* 53, 3: 149–156.
Service, E. 1992. Phonology, working memory, and foreign language learning. *The Quarterly Journal of Experimental Psychology* 45A 1: 21–50.
Service, E. and Kohonen, V. 1995. Is the relation between phonological memory and foreign language learning accounted for by vocabulary acquisition? *Applied Psycholinguistics* 16: 155–172.
Sharwood Smith, M. 1981. Consciousness-raising and the second language learner. *Applied Linguistics* 2, 2: 159–168.
Sheen, R. 1992. Problem solving brought to task. *RELC Journal* 23, 2: 44–59.
Simcock, M. 1993. Developing productive vocabulary using the "Ask and answer" technique. *Guidelines* 15, 1–7.
Simpson, A. 1981. Interviews between native speakers and non-native speakers as material for listening comprehension. *ELT Journal* 35, 4: 372–375.
Singleton, D. 1999. *Exploring the Second Language Mental Lexicon.* Cambridge: Cambridge University Press.
Skehan, P. 1998. *A Cognitive Approach to Language Learning.* Oxford: Oxford University Press.
Spada, N. 1997. Form-focussed instruction and second language acquisition: a review of classroom and laboratory research. *Language Teaching* 30: 73–87.
Stahl, S.A. and Vancil, S.J. 1986. Discussion is what makes semantic maps work in vocabulary instruction. *The Reading Teacher* 40, 1: 62–67.
Stenstrom, A. 1990. Lexical items perculiar to spoken discourse. In J. Svartik (ed.), *The London-Lund Corpus of Spoken English: Description and Research, Lund Studies in English 82* (pp. 137–175). Lund: Lund University Press.
Stevick, E.W. 1978. Toward a practical philosophy of pronunciation: another view. *TESOL Quarterly* 12, 2: 145–150.
Strevens, P. 1974. A rationale for teaching pronunciation: the rival virtues of innocence and sophistication. *ELT Journal* 28, 3: 182–189.
Swain, M. 1985. Communicative competence: some roles of comprehensible input and comprehensible output in its development. In S. Gass and C. Madden (eds), *Input in Second Language Acquisition* (pp. 235–253). Rowley, Mass.: Newbury House.
Swain, M. 1995. Three functions of output in second language learning. In G. Cook and B. Seidelhofer (eds), *Principle and Practice in Applied Linguistics: Studies in Honour of H.G. Widdowson* (pp. 125–144). Oxford: Oxford University Press.
Swain, M. 2000. The output hypothesis and beyond: mediating acquisition through collaborative dialogue. In J. Lantolf (ed.), *Sociocultural Theory and Second Language Learning* (pp. 97–119). Oxford: Oxford University Press.
Swain, M. 2005. The output hypothesis: theory and research. In E. Hinkel (ed.), *Handbook of*

196 • References

Research in Second Language Teaching and Learning (pp. 471–483). Mahwah, N.J.: Lawrence Erlbaum Associates.

Swain, M. and Lapkin, S. 1998. Interaction and second language learning: Two adolescent French immersion students working together. *Modern Language Journal* 82, 320–337.

Tahta, S., Wood, M. and Lowenthal, K. 1981a. Age changes in the ability to replicate foreign pronunciation and intonation. *Language and Speech* 24, 4: 363–372.

Tahta, S., Wood, M. and Lowenthal, K. 1981b. Foreign accents: factors relating to transfer of accent from the first language to the second language. *Language and Speech* 24, 3: 265–272.

Tauroza, S. and Allison, D. 1990. Speech rates in British English. *Applied Linguistics* 11, 1: 90–105.

Taylor, B.P. 1982. In search of real reality. *TESOL Quarterly* 16, 1: 28–42.

Templeton, H. 1977. A new technique for measuring listening comprehension. *ELT Journal* 31, 4: 292–299.

Terrell, T.D. 1982. The natural approach to language teaching: an update. *Modern Language Journal* 66, 2: 121–132.

Thomas, G.I. and Nation, I.S.P. 1979. Communicating through the ordering exercise. *Guidelines* 1: 68–75.

Thornbury, S. 2001. *Uncovering Grammar*. Oxford: Macmillan Heinemann.

Thornbury, S. 2005. *How to Teach Speaking*. Essex: Pearson.

Thorndike, E.L. 1908. Memory for paired associates. *Psychological Review* 15, 122–138.

Tinkham, T, 1993. The effect of semantic clustering on the learning of second language vocabulary. *System* 21, 3: 371–380.

Tinkham, T. 1997. The effects of semantic and thematic clustering on the learning of second language vocabulary. *Second Language Research* 13, 2: 138–163.

Todd, S. C. 1996. Why we should stop teaching our students to take notes: evidence that the "encoding hypothesis" isn't right. In C. Reves, C. Steele, and C.S.P. Wong (eds), *Linguistics and Language Teaching: Proceedings of the sixth joint LSH-HATESL conference* (pp. 201–222). Honolulu: University of Hawai'i, Second Language Teaching and Curriculum Center (Technical Report #10).

Tomasello, M. and Herron, C. 1989. Feedback for language transfer errors: the garden path technique. *SSLA* 11: 385–396.

Trofimovich, P. and Gatbonton, E. 2006. Repetition and focus on form in processing L2 Spanish words: implications for pronunciation instruction. *Modern Language Journal* 90, 4: 519–535.

Tsui, A. and Fullilove, J. 1998. Bottom-up or top-down processing as a discriminator of L2 listening performance. *Applied Linguistics* 19, 4: 432–451.

Tucker, C.A. 1972. Programmed dictation: an example of the P.I. process in the classroom. *TESOL Quarterly* 6, 1: 61–70.

Ur, P. 1981. *Discussions that Work*. Cambridge: Cambridge University Press.

van Ek, J.A. and Alexander, L.G. 1980. *Threshold Level English*. Oxford: Pergamon Press.

van Moere, A. 2006. Validity evidence in a university group oral test. *Language Testing* 23, 4: 411–440.

Wajnryb, R. 1988. The Dicto-gloss method of language teaching: a text-based communicative approach to grammar. *English Teaching Forum* 26, 3: 35–38.

Wajnryb, R. 1989. Dicto-gloss: a text-based communicative approach to teaching and learning grammar. *English Teaching Forum* 27, 4: 16–19.

Wajnryb, R. 1990. *Grammar Dictations*. Oxford: Oxford University Press.

Walker, C. 1990. Large-scale oral testing. *Applied Linguistics* 11, 2: 200–219.

Waring, R. 1997. The negative effects of learning words in semantic sets: a replication. *System* 25, 2: 261–274.

Waring, R. and Takaki, M. 2003. At what rate do learners learn and retain new vocabulary from reading a graded reader? *Reading in a Foreign Language* 15, 2: 130–163.

Watts, N.R. 1986. Developing aural anticipation and prediction strategies. *English Teaching Forum* 24, 1: 21–23, 29.

Webb, S. 2002. *Investigating the effects of learning tasks on vocabulary knowledge*. PhD thesis, Victoria University of Wellington.

Webb, S. 2005. Receptive and productive vocabulary learning: The effects of reading and writing on word knowledge. *SSLA*, 27, 33–52.

Webb, W.B. 1962. The effects of prolonged learning on learning. *Journal of Verbal Learning and Verbal Behavior* 1, 173–182.

West, M.P. 1941. *Learning to Read a Foreign Language and Other Essays*. London: Longman.

West, M.P. 1953. *A General Service List of English Words*. London: Longman.

West, M.P. 1960. *Teaching English in Difficult Circumstances*. London: Longman.

White, R.V. 1978. Teaching the passive. *ELT Journal* 32, 3: 188–193.

Whiteson, V. 1978. Testing pronunciation in the language laboratory. *ELT Journal* 33, 1: 30–31.

Williams, J. 2005. Form-focused instruction. In E. Hinkel (ed.), *Handbook of Research in Second Language Teaching and Learning* (pp. 671–691). Mahwah, N.J.: Lawrence Erlbaum Associates.

Willis, J. 1996. *Exposure to Spontaneous Speech Using Recordings. A Framework for Task-Based Learning*. London: Longman.

Wilson, M. 2003. Discovery listening: improving perceptual processing. *ELT Journal* 57, 4: 335–343.

Winitz, H. (ed.) 1981. *The Comprehension Approach to Foreign Language Instruction*. Rowley, Mass.: Newbury House.

Wintz, H. and Bellarose, B. 1965. Phoneme-cluster learning as a function of instructional method and age. *Journal of Verbal Learning and Verbal Behavior* 4: 98–102.

Wood, D. 2006. Uses and functions of formulaic sequences in second language speech. *Canadian Modern Language Review* 63, 1: 13–33.

Wu, Y. 1998. What do tests of listening comprehension test? A retrospection study of EFL test-takers performing a multiple-choice task. *Language Testing* 15: 21–44.

Yashima, T. 2002. Willingness to communicate in a second language: the Japanese EFL context. *The Modern Language Journal* 86, 1: 54–66.

Yasui, M. no date. *Consonant Patterning in English*. Tokyo: Kenkyushu.

Yuan, F. and Ellis, R. 2003. The effects of pre-task planning and on-line planning on fluency, complexity and accuracy in L2 monologic oral production. *Applied Linguistics* 24, 1: 1–27.

Techniques Index

Index

read and-look-up 66
recorded cloze 170
rehearsed talks 162
reliability 166–7
remedial work 143
repeating sounds 87
reproduction exercise 71
responding to statements 170
retelling 70, 118, 121
role plays 175–6
running dictation 59, 62

same or different 32, 44–5, 154
self-assessment 165
self-checking pair work 139
sentence dictation 65
short turns 117
slurring and bracketing 88
sound dictation 87
split information 101, 165, 172
stage 1, 2 and 3 questions 31
stress 90–2
strip story 105–6
substitution tables 24, 112
surveys 27–8
survival vocabulary 10, 18, 166,
    179–82

testing the teacher 88
text with questions 170
three choice true false 170
time-on-task 2
tongue twisters 82
top-down 40, 158
transactional listening 40
transformation exercises 138–9
triads 125
triplets 86–7
twenty questions 31

unexploded dictation 65
using the written forms 88–9

validity 167–8
visit and listen 160
vocabulary 132–7
vocabulary cards 135

walk and talk 32
washback 169
what is it? 26, 33, 34, 44, 112
word detectives 137
word part analysis 135

you said . . . 119